The Private Pay Practitioners Playbook

Systems, Scripts & Strategies for Financial Freedom in Private Pay Practice

D.J. Burr, LMHC, LPC

First Edition

ISBN:979-8-9999285-1-1

Printed in the United States of America

Disclaimer

The information contained in this book is for educational and informational purposes only. It is not intended as a substitute for professional consultation, supervision, or legal advice. The strategies and techniques described are based on the author's experience and should be adapted to individual circumstances and local regulations.

The author makes no representations or warranties with respect to the accuracy or completeness of the contents of this book and specifically disclaims any implied warranties of merchantability or fitness for a particular purpose. The advice and strategies contained herein may not be suitable for every situation.

Neither the author nor the publisher shall be liable for any loss of profit or any other commercial damages, including but not limited to special, incidental, consequential, or other damages, arising from the use of information in this book.

Readers are encouraged to consult with appropriate licensed professionals regarding their specific business and clinical practices.

Contact Information

For more resources and information:

- Website: www.djburr.com
- Patreon: patreon.com/privatepay
- Facebook: Private Pay Practitioners & Black Private Pay Practitioners

Table of Contents

- Handling Difficult Endings

Chapter 9: Scaling Your Impact

- Building a Practice That Serves Your Life
- The Fall Launch Advantage
- Creating Seasonal Growth Patterns
- Systems That Scale
- Creating Multiple Revenue Streams
- Building Your Legacy Practice
- Implementation: Your 90-Day Launch Plan

Conclusion

About the Author

Appendix:

Resource Library for Private Pay Success
- **Appendix A:** Assessment & Planning Tools
- **Appendix B:** Marketing & Networking Templates
- **Appendix C:** Implementation Checklists
- **Appendix D:** Business Systems Templates

Introduction

If you picked up this book, chances are you're tired of something. Maybe you're tired of insurance hassles, tired of being told what you can and can't do in your sessions, tired of working harder but not earning what you're worth. Maybe you're just tired of settling for a practice that doesn't match your vision of what therapy should be.

I get it. I've been exactly where you are.

This isn't another theoretical guide written by someone who's never actually built a practice. Everything in this book comes from real experience - my journey from community mental health to private practice, the hundreds of therapists I've consulted with through the transition, and the thousands of conversations I've had with practitioners who've made private pay work.

Why This Book Exists

The mental health field is full of incredibly skilled therapists who struggle to build sustainable practices. Not because they lack clinical expertise, but because nobody taught them the business side of private practice. Graduate school prepared you to be a therapist, not a business owner.

This book bridges that gap.

It's the guide I wish I'd had when I was making the transition. It's the resource my consultation clients ask for after our calls. It's the compilation of strategies, systems, and scripts that work in the real world.

My Story (The Short Version)

I began my career in community mental health, transitioning to a shared office space with other therapists. However, I scaled too quickly, expanding to multiple locations and staff, which led to overwhelm and a subsequent downsizing. Following this, I worked from home for a period before moving to a solo office. Ultimately, I found my niche in private pay practice.

That journey taught me what works and what doesn't. More importantly, it taught me that there's no single "right" way to build a practice. The right way is the way that aligns with your values, serves your ideal clients, and creates the life you want.

I learned that private pay isn't about being elitist or greedy. It's about creating sustainable practices that allow us to do our best work while building lives we enjoy living.

What Makes This Different

Most business books for therapists are either too generic ("build your brand!") or too tactical ("here's how to set up QuickBooks"). This book gives you both the strategic framework and the practical tools.

You'll get:

- **Clear decision-making frameworks** for every significant choice you'll face
- **Word-for-word scripts** for difficult conversations
- **Step-by-step implementation guides** for everything from networking to launching groups
- **Real case studies** from actual therapists (anonymized, of course)
- **Templates and worksheets** you can use immediately
- **Seasonal strategies** that work with natural rhythms rather than against them

How to Use This Book

This book is designed to be practical, not theoretical. Each chapter builds on the previous one, but you can also jump to specific sections as needed.

If you're considering private pay, please read it through.

If you're already in private practice but struggling with specific areas (like marketing or networking), jump to those chapters.

The appendix contains all the templates and tools referenced throughout the book. Print them out, customize them to your style, and start using them immediately.

The Fall Advantage

There's a reason I'm encouraging you to implement these strategies this fall. September through November is consistently the highest-demand period for mental health services. People return from summer with renewed focus, students and families settle into routines, and there's a collective "fresh start" energy in the air.

If you're going to make this transition, fall gives you the best chance of success. The market is favorable, motivation is high, and you can build momentum that carries through the busy winter months.

What You Can Expect

By the time you finish this book and implement its
strategies, you'll have:

- **Crystal clear messaging** that attracts your ideal clients
- **Systems and processes** that make your practice run
  smoothly
- **A professional network** that generates consistent
  referrals
- **Pricing confidence** based on value, not fear
- **Multiple service delivery options** beyond traditional
  therapy
- **Time management strategies** that prevent burnout
- **A 90-day implementation plan** for fall launch

More importantly, you'll have a practice that
serves your life instead of dominating it.

A Note on Ethics

Everything in this book is designed to help you build an
ethical, sustainable practice that serves your clients well.
Making money and doing good work aren't mutually
exclusive - in fact, therapists who are financially
sustainable tend to provide better care because they're

not stressed about their survival.

Private pay doesn't mean serving only wealthy clients. It means charging appropriately for your expertise so you can afford to offer sliding scale spots, pro bono work, or other ways of serving your community.

My Promise to You

I promise to give you strategies that work, not just theories that sound good. I promise to be honest about what's hard and what's not. I promise to provide tools you can implement immediately, not concepts you have to figure out on your own.

Most importantly, I promise to help you build a practice that aligns with your values and supports the life you want to live.

Your Promise to Yourself

Before you dive in, make a promise to yourself: you'll implement at least one strategy from this book within the next week. Not next month, not when you have more time, but this week.

The key difference between therapists who successfully transition to private pay and those who merely consider it lies in action—small, consistent actions compound into significant results.

Let's Begin

You already have everything you need to build a successful private pay practice. You have clinical skills, life experience, and something unique to offer. What you might be missing is a business framework that packages and presents your work in a way that attracts your ideal clients and sustains you professionally.

That's what this book provides.

The mental health field needs more therapists who understand their worth and create practices that model sustainability and excellence. Your success doesn't just serve you - it serves everyone who needs what you have to offer and every therapist who needs to see that this is possible.

Private pay isn't a dream. It's a decision.

"You already have everything you need to build a successful private pay practice. You have clinical skills, life experience, and something unique to offer. What you might be missing is the business framework to package and present what you do."

Getting Started Action Steps:

✓ Make a promise to implement ONE strategy within the next week
✓ Identify your biggest barrier to private pay transition
✓ Connect with one other therapist making this journey
✓ Read this book with a pen in hand - make it interactive

Chapter 1: The Private Pay Decision

Introduction

Let me tell you something that might surprise you: private pay isn't a dream. It's a decision.

I know, I know. You've probably heard all the reasons why you "should" take insurance. You've been told it's more ethical, that you're serving those who need it most, that it's the responsible thing to do. I've heard it all too. But here's what I've learned after years in this field and helping hundreds of therapists make this transition: those are myths that keep good therapists stuck in systems that don't serve them or their clients well.

This book isn't about convincing you to go private pay. You're already here, which means part of you knows this is the direction you want to go. This book provides you with a roadmap to achieve success.

Why Private Pay? Why Now?

Every therapist I work with has their own story about what brought them to consider private pay. Maybe you're exhausted by insurance paperwork. Perhaps you're tired of having your clinical decisions questioned by people who've never sat across from a client in crisis. You may want to create the kind of therapeutic experience you know your clients deserve.

Or maybe you've realized that the current system isn't sustainable for anyone - not for therapists, and not for the clients we're trying to serve.

Whatever brought you here, you're in good company. The therapists who make this transition successfully aren't necessarily the most experienced or the most credentialed. They're the ones who get clear on their why, take systematic action, and commit to building something better.

The Myths That Keep Us Stuck

Myth #1: "Taking insurance is more ethical because you're helping people who can't afford therapy."

Here's the reality: when you're overwhelmed, underpaid, and burning out from insurance hassles, you're not helping anyone to the best of your capacity. The therapist who charges appropriately, works with ideal clients, and has the energy to be fully present is providing better care than the one who's spread too thin.

Plus, many insurance-based therapists end up with caseloads full of people who aren't fully invested in the work because they're not making a financial commitment. There's something powerful about investment - both economic and emotional.

Myth #2: "I need to be an expert to charge private pay rates."

You don't need to be the world's leading authority on your niche. You need to be good at what you do and clear about who you serve. The therapist who has practiced for three years but has a clear specialty and firm boundaries often outperforms the one with twenty years of experience who takes on anyone and tries to be everything to everyone.

Myth #3: "There aren't enough people who can afford private pay therapy."

This one always makes me laugh. Millions of people spend money on life coaches, wellness programs, expensive gym memberships, and designer coffee every month. The issue isn't whether people have money - it's whether they see the value in what you're offering and whether you're reaching the right people.

Case Study: A Strategic Transition

Let me tell you about a therapist in the Midwest who came to me for consultation. When I first connected with her, she had been in practice for eight years and was juggling contracts with multiple insurance panels. She specialized in anxiety and depression, but felt like she was constantly drowning in paperwork and prior authorization requests.

Her situation was all too familiar:

- Working 50+ hours per week, but taking home less than she made as a hospital counselor
- Spending evenings and weekends on insurance documentation
- Feeling frustrated that sessions were dictated by what insurance would cover rather than what clients needed
- Considering leaving the field entirely because the stress was affecting her mental health

The breaking point came when one insurance company

terminated her contract with just 30 days' notice, leaving her scrambling to help existing clients. She realized she was building her career on an unstable foundation, leaving her with no control.

She decided to transition to private pay, but she did it strategically. She gave her existing insurance clients six months' notice and focused on building her private pay caseload during that time. She clarified her specialization in anxiety disorders for working professionals and crafted messaging that spoke directly to that population.

The results? Within eight months of her full transition:

• Her income increased by 40% while working fewer hours
• She had a waitlist of ideal clients who valued her expertise
•Sunday anxiety about the upcoming work week completely disappeared
• She remembered why she became a therapist in the first place

Her story isn't unique. It's the same pattern I see with therapist after therapist who makes this transition thoughtfully and systematically.

What This Book Will Do for You

This isn't a theoretical guide written by someone who's never built a practice. Everything in here comes from real experience - my transition from community mental health to private practice, and the hundreds of therapists I've consulted with who've made this leap successfully.

You're going to get:

- **Clear frameworks** for identifying your ideal clients and crafting messaging that attracts them
- **Step-by-step systems** for consultations that convert without feeling salesy
- **Networking strategies** that work (and don't make you feel gross)
- **Pricing guidance** based on value, not just time
- **Templates and scripts** you can use immediately
- **Case studies** from real therapists who've done this successfully

Most importantly, you'll receive a roadmap designed to work for both those just starting and those with decades of experience in practice.

The Fall Advantage

There's a reason I'm encouraging you to launch this fall, and it's not just about arbitrary timing. Fall is prime time for mental health professionals. Think about it:

• People are returning from summer with renewed focus and energy
• Students and families are settling into new routines
• There's a collective "fresh start" energy in the air
•Adults are thinking about what they want to change or improve
•The holiday season is approaching, which often brings up family and relationship issues

September through November consistently see the highest demand for therapy services. If you're going to make this transition, why not time it when the market is most favorable?

Your Decision Point

Here's what I want you to know: you already have everything you need to build a successful private pay practice. You have clinical skills, life experience, and something unique to offer. What you might be missing is a business framework to package and present your services in a way that attracts your ideal clients.

That's what this book provides.

The decision isn't really whether you're "ready" for private pay. The decision is whether you're ready to stop settling for a practice that doesn't serve you or your clients well, and start building something that does.

So let me ask you: what are you no longer willing to tolerate in your practice? What would need to change for you to feel excited about Monday mornings again? What kind of therapist do you want to be when you're not exhausted by insurance hassles and administrative burdens?

Your answers to those questions are the beginning of your private pay journey.

What's Coming Next

In the next chapter, we'll clarify your why and who - the foundation that everything else builds on. Because here's the thing: successful private pay practices aren't built on desperation or generic marketing. They're built on clarity.

Clarity about who you serve, what you offer, and why

you're uniquely positioned to help. When you have that clarity, everything else - the marketing, the networking, the consultations - becomes so much easier.

Ready to get started?

"Private pay isn't a dream. It's a decision. The key difference between therapists who successfully transition to private pay and those who merely consider it lies in action. Small, consistent actions compound into significant results."

Chapter Action Steps:

✓ Identify which myth is keeping you stuck in insurance panels
✓ Write down your #1 reason for considering private pay
✓ Schedule 2 hours this week to start your transition planning
✓ Join one private pay practitioner community or resource

Chapter 2: Know Your Why & Your Who

The Foundation That Changes Everything

Here's what I see happen all the time: therapists jump into private pay with a generic website that says they help "individuals struggling with anxiety, depression, and life transitions." Their About page talks about their credentials and theoretical orientations. They wonder why they're not getting calls.

The problem isn't their clinical skills. The problem is they haven't done the foundational work of getting clear on their why and their who. Without this clarity, you're just another therapist in a sea of therapists. With it, you become the obvious choice for your ideal clients.

This chapter will walk you through the exact process I use with every therapist I consult with. It's the same process that transformed my practice and the practices of hundreds of others. By the end of this chapter, you'll have a clear niche statement, messaging that converts, and a *deep understanding of who you're meant to serve.*

Starting With Your Why

Before we talk about who you want to work with, we need to get clear on why you're doing this work. And I don't mean the surface-level answer about wanting to help people. I mean the deep, personal why that makes this more than just a job for you.

I learned this lesson the hard way. When I first moved from community mental health to private practice, I tried to be everything to everyone. I thought that's what you were supposed to do - cast a wide net, take anyone who called. But I was miserable, and my practice felt scattered.

It wasn't until I got honest about my recovery journey and how that shaped my understanding of change and healing that everything clicked into place. Suddenly, I wasn't just another therapist - I was someone who understood the specific challenges my ideal clients were facing because I'd walked a similar path.

Grounding in Purpose Exercise

Take a few minutes to think about these questions:

What drew you to private pay specifically?

- *What are you no longer willing to tolerate in your business?*
- *What model of practice aligns with your values?*
- *What kind of therapeutic relationship do you want to create?*

What lived experiences or values make you uniquely positioned to serve specific clients? *This is where many therapists get uncomfortable, but here's the truth: your personal experiences - when used ethically and appropriately - can be your greatest clinical asset. They don't make you unprofessional; they make you human and relatable.*

How do clients experience you differently from other providers?

- *What do people often thank you for?*
- *What do they say they remember about working with you?*
- *What comes naturally to you in the therapeutic relationship?*

My Journey: Finding Your Niche Through Experience

I remember sitting in that shared office space - you know, the kind where multiple therapists rent rooms and you swap spaces between sessions - wondering how to position myself. I had this powerful recovery story, but I was terrified to use it professionally. What if people thought I was unprofessional? What if they questioned my ability to help them?

For years, I tried to be the neutral, blank-slate therapist I learned about in graduate school. I thought that's what professionalism looked like. But I was miserable, and my practice felt scattered.

The shift happened when I realized my recovery experience wasn't something to hide from - it was precisely what made me the right therapist for certain clients. I started offering a free chapter of my memoir on my website. Not because I wanted people to see me as their sponsor, but because I wanted them to know they weren't alone in their struggle. That single decision changed everything about how people connected with my work.

Here's how my practice transformed:

Before getting clear on my why:

- *Generic website that could apply to any therapist*
- *Inconsistent referrals from colleagues who weren't sure what I specialized in*
- *Consultation calls with people who weren't ready for the work*
- *Constant questioning of whether I was qualified enough*

After embracing my unique positioning:

- *Clear messaging about my expertise with addiction and recovery*
- *Referrals from professionals who knew exactly what I offered*
- *Consultation calls with people who said they specifically wanted someone who understood their experience*
- *Confidence in my expertise and unique value*

My recovery story wasn't the primary focus of therapy sessions, but it shaped my approach, deepened my understanding, and enhanced my ability to connect authentically with clients facing similar challenges. It made me the right therapist for my ideal clients.

Getting Clear on Your Ideal Client

Now that you're grounded in your why, let's talk about your who. This is where the Ideal Client Clarity framework comes in. I've used this with hundreds of therapists, and it never fails to create those lightbulb moments.

The Deep Dive Questions

What keeps your ideal client up at night? *I'm not talking about their diagnosis. I'm talking about the 3 AM thoughts, the worries that cycle through their mind, the fears that feel too embarrassing to say out loud.*

What are they afraid will happen if nothing changes? *This is where you tap into the real motivation for change. People don't seek therapy because everything is fine. They seek therapy because they're afraid of where their current path is leading.*

What do they want most in life, relationships, or therapy? *Again, go deeper than symptom reduction.*

What do they want their life to look like? What kind of person do they want to be? What kind of relationships do they want to have?

What do they believe about themselves that might be getting in the way? *These are the limiting beliefs, the negative self-talk, the stories they tell themselves that keep them stuck.*

What makes them feel seen, safe, or empowered? *This is crucial for understanding how to create the therapeutic environment they need.*

What They Say vs. What They Need

Here's one of my favorite exercises because it cuts right to the heart of effective marketing and clinical work. Complete these sentences:

- *They say they want _____, but they really need _____.*
- *They think the problem is _____, but the real challenge is _____.*
- *For example:*
  - *They claim they want to stop feeling anxious, but what they need to do is learn to trust themselves again.*

- *They think the problem is their panic attacks, but the real challenge is the perfectionism that's driving their anxiety.*

This distinction is everything. When you can speak to what they need (not just what they think they want), your messaging becomes magnetic to the right people.

Case Study: From Generic to Magnetic

I've seen this transformation countless times in my consultations. One therapist came to me with a technically successful practice - she was booked solid - but she was miserable. She was seeing anyone who called, which meant her days were full of people she didn't particularly enjoy working with and problems she wasn't especially passionate about solving.

Through our work together, she completed the ideal client clarity exercise and realized she lit up when talking about working with women entrepreneurs struggling with perfectionism. Within three months of getting clear and updating her messaging, referrals for women entrepreneurs increased dramatically, her consultation calls became easier, and her energy for her work returned.

The lesson? She didn't become a different therapist. She became a clearer therapist - clear about who she served best and why.

Your Voice and Positioning

Once you know your why and your who, you need to think about your voice. How do you naturally communicate? What tone feels authentic to you?

Finding Your Natural Voice

What kind of tone do you naturally speak or write in?

- *Calm and reassuring?*
- *Bold and direct?*
- *Nurturing and gentle?*
- *Straightforward and practical?*

There's no right answer here. The goal is authenticity, not trying to be someone you're not.

What are 2-3 things you stand for in your work?
These are your non-negotiables, the principles that guide how you practice. For example:

- *Therapy should be collaborative, not prescriptive*

- *Healing happens in a relationship, not in isolation*

- *People are the experts on their own lives*

What are 1-2 things you actively reject?
Sometimes it's easier to define yourself by what you're not. This helps ideal clients self-select and non-ideal clients self-select out.

What do people often thank you for or say they remember about you? *Pay attention to the feedback you get. Clients will tell you what your superpowers are if you listen.*

Putting It All Together: Your Messaging Framework

Now we're going to take everything you've discovered and turn it into clear, compelling messaging. This becomes the foundation for your website, your networking conversations, your consultation calls - everything.

The Formula That Works

Try completing these statements:

**I help _____ who are _____
so they can_____.**

For example:

- *I help high-achieving women who are burned out from perfectionism so they can find sustainable success without sacrificing their well-being.*
- *I help men in their 30s and 40s who feel disconnected from their emotions so they can build deeper, more authentic relationships.*

Clients don't hire me for _____, they hire me for _____.

This helps distinguish between surface-level presenting issues and more profound transformation.

The real reason people stay with me is because _____.

This speaks to your unique value and therapeutic style.

My work isn't for everyone — and that's a good thing because _____.

This helps you embrace your niche instead

of trying to be everything to everyone.

Case Study: The Power of Authentic Positioning

Here's another example from my consultation work. One therapist was initially hesitant to share his experience with grief in his professional position. He worried it would make him seem unprofessional or like he hadn't "done his work."

Through our work together, he gradually began incorporating his understanding of grief from both professional and personal perspectives. The difference was immediate - clients began saying they chose him specifically because he genuinely understood and empathized with their experience, and his confidence in sessions increased because he was working in his area of genuine expertise. He knew his story. And he understood theirs.

He learned what I learned years ago: lived experience doesn't make you less professional - it makes you more human and more effective with the clients you're meant to serve.

Making It Real: Your Practice Prompts

Before you move on to the next chapter, spend some time with these prompts:

1. **Write out your one-sentence niche statement** *using the formula: "I help [who] with [what] so they can [result]."*

2. **Identify your unique positioning.** *What combination of experience, training, and personal qualities makes you the right therapist for your ideal clients?*

3. **Craft your elevator pitch.** *How would you introduce yourself at a networking event in 30 seconds or less?*

4. **Define your ideal client's journey.** *What brings them to therapy? What are they hoping will be different in six months?*

5. **Clarify your boundaries.** *What types of clients or issues energize you vs. drain you?*

What's Coming Next

In the next chapter, we'll leverage your newfound clarity to craft messaging that drives conversions. We'll cover everything from website copy that attracts ideal clients to consultation call scripts that feel authentic and effective.

I'll share the exact templates and scripts I've developed through years of building my practice and consulting with hundreds of others. These aren't theoretical frameworks - they're battle-tested strategies that have helped therapists go from crickets on their website to waitlists of ideal clients.

The difference between therapists who struggle to fill their practices and those who have more referrals than they can handle often comes down to one thing: the ability to communicate their value. Let's make sure you're in the second group.

Chapter Action Steps:

✓ Complete: "I help _____ who are _____ so they can _____"
✓ Identify your unique positioning (experience + training + personal qualities)
✓ Write your 30-second elevator pitch
✓ Define what energizes vs. drains you in client work

Chapter 3: Messaging That Converts

From Clarity to Connection

You've done the hard work of getting clear on your why and your who. Now comes the part where many therapists get stuck: translating that clarity into messaging that attracts ideal clients and converts consultation calls into paying clients.

I learned this lesson early in my transition to private pay. I had figured out my niche and felt confident about my expertise, but my website still sounded like every other therapist's website. My consultation calls felt awkward because I struggled to discuss my services without coming across as "selling." And don't even get me started on networking - I had no idea what to say when people asked what I did.

The breakthrough came when I realized that effective messaging isn't about being salesy or promotional. It's about being clear, authentic, and speaking directly to the experience of the people you want to serve. When you get this right, marketing stops feeling like marketing and starts feeling like a connection.

The Website That Works

Your website is often the first impression potential clients have of you. Most therapist websites make the same mistakes: they focus on credentials instead of outcomes, use clinical jargon instead of human language, and try to appeal to everyone instead of speaking directly to their ideal clients.

The Homepage Formula That Converts

Here's the structure I've tested with hundreds of therapists:

Opening Statement (What you do + who for):
Instead of "I provide individual therapy for adults," try: "I help high-achieving professionals who look successful on paper but feel empty inside create authentic lives that align with their values."

The Problem You Solve: *Speak directly to their 3 AM thoughts: "You've checked all the boxes - good job, nice house, solid relationship - but you wake up feeling like you're living someone else's life. You're exhausted from pretending everything is fine when inside you feel disconnected from what matters to you."*

Your Unique Approach: This is where your lived experience and clinical expertise come together: "Having navigated my journey from achievement addiction to authentic living, I understand both the external pressures and internal struggles that keep successful people stuck in unfulfilling patterns."

What Changes: Paint a picture of their life after working with you: "Imagine waking up excited about your day, making decisions from your values instead of others' expectations, and feeling genuinely connected to the life you're building."

Clear Next Step: Make it easy to take action: "Ready to start living authentically? Schedule a free 20-minute consultation to see if we're a good fit."

My Website Evolution

When I first went private pay, my website focused solely on my credentials and theoretical orientation. It could have described any therapist. The transformation occurred when I began sharing my story authentically.

I added that free chapter from my memoir - not as a marketing gimmick, but because I genuinely wanted people to know they weren't alone in their struggle. That single addition changed everything. Suddenly, people were calling and saying, "I read your story and I knew you'd understand what I'm going through."

The lesson? Your website should be a conversation with your ideal client, not a resume for a licensing board.

Consultation Calls That Convert

This is where most therapists either undersell themselves or oversell themselves. The key is finding that sweet spot where you're confident about your expertise while remaining collaborative and client-focused.

The Structure That Works

I've refined this consultation structure through hundreds of calls:

Opening (2-3 minutes): "Thanks for taking the time to talk today. I have about 20 minutes to get to know you and see if we might be a good fit to work together. Before we dive in, what's prompting you to consider therapy right now?"

Understanding Their World (8-10 minutes): Ask questions that help you understand both their presenting concerns and their deeper motivations:

- *What would need to change for you to feel like therapy was successful?* ● *Have you worked with a therapist before? What was helpful or not helpful about that experience?*
- *What are you hoping will be different in your life six months from now?*

Sharing Your Approach (5-7 minutes): *"Based on what you're sharing, it sounds like you're dealing with [reflect their core concerns]. I work with a lot of people facing similar challenges. My approach focuses on [brief description that connects to their needs]. What I find most effective is [key elements that differentiate you]."*

Logistics and Fit (3-5 minutes): *"Let me share how I work: I see clients weekly for 50-minute sessions. I'm a private-pay practice, which means you pay at the time of service, and I can provide a superbill for potential insurance reimbursement. My rate is $X per session. What questions do you have about the logistics?"*

Next Steps: *If it feels like a good fit: "This sounds like work we could definitely do together. Would you like to schedule our first session?"*

If it doesn't feel like a fit: "Based on what you're sharing, I think you'd benefit from someone who specializes more specifically in [area]. I'd be happy to provide some referrals."

What I Learned From My Consultation Calls

Early on, I made the mistake of spending consultation calls trying to convince people to work with me. I'd oversell my credentials and undersell my rates. The shift happened when I realized that consultation calls aren't about persuasion - they're about mutual assessment.

Now I approach every consultation call with genuine curiosity about whether we're a good fit. This confidence comes across and actually makes people more likely to want to work with me. When you're clear about who you serve best, you can have these conversations from a place of abundance rather than desperation.

Case Study: From Crickets to Waitlist

Let me tell you about a therapist who came to me because her website was getting traffic but not generating calls. She had good SEO and professional photos, but something wasn't connecting.

The problem became obvious when I looked at her homepage. It was all clinical language and vague promises. Her target audience was "adults struggling with anxiety and depression," which describes about 80% of potential therapy clients.

Here's what we changed:

Before: *"I provide evidence-based treatment for anxiety and depression using cognitive-behavioral and mindfulness-based approaches."*

After: *"I help women in their 30s and 40s who are exhausted from trying to be perfect at everything learn to set boundaries and prioritize their own well-being without guilt."*

Before: *Generic stock photo of a peaceful office*

After: *A warm, authentic photo with a bio that mentioned her own experience with perfectionism and people-pleasing*

Before: *"Contact me to schedule an appointment."*

After: *"Ready to stop putting everyone else's needs before your own? Let's talk."*

The results were immediate. Within two weeks, she went from getting one or two inquiries per month to getting multiple calls per week from women who said variations of "I felt like you were speaking directly to me."

The Power of Storytelling

One of the most powerful tools in your messaging arsenal is story. Not just your personal story (though that can be incredibly valuable when used appropriately), but the stories of transformation you witness in your work.

Using Your Story Ethically

I get asked about this a lot: How do you use your personal experience in your professional messaging without making it about you?

Here's what I've learned from years of sharing my recovery story in my practice:
Do:
- *Share your story when it serves the client's need to feel understood*
- *Focus on universal themes (struggle, change, growth) rather than specific details*
- *Use it to illustrate that change is possible, not to prove your credibility*
- *Be mindful of timing and context*

Don't:

- *Make the session about your experience*

- *Share details that serve your need to be seen rather than their need to be helped • Use your story as proof that you're the only one who can help them*

- *Assume your path is the right path for everyone*

The key is discernment. Your story can be a powerful tool for connection and hope, but it should always serve the therapeutic relationship, not your ego.

Seasonal Messaging That Works

One of the advantages of launching in the fall is that you can tap into the natural "fresh start" energy that comes with the season. Here are some messaging approaches that work particularly well in September and October:

"Back to Therapy" Messaging: *"September feels like a natural reset, doesn't it? If you've been considering starting therapy, now might be the perfect time. Fall energy brings clarity about what we want to change and the motivation to* take action."

Transition Themes: "Fall transitions can bring up so much - excitement, anxiety, grief for summer, anticipation for what's ahead. If you're feeling overwhelmed by change or unsure about your next steps, you don't have to figure it out alone."

Holiday Preparation: "The holiday season is approaching, and with it often comes family stress, relationship dynamics, and old patterns. What if this year could be different?"

My Fall Launch Strategy

When I decided to expand my practice offerings, I intentionally scheduled the launch for early fall. I crafted messaging around the themes of "investing in yourself this fall" and "using the natural energy of the season for personal growth."

The response was incredible. People resonated with the timing and the message. It felt aligned rather than forced, seasonal rather than sales-driven.

Social Media That Feels Authentic

Most therapists either avoid social media entirely or post

generic mental health tips that could come from anyone. There's a middle ground that works much better: authentic, educational content that showcases your personality and expertise.

Content Ideas That Convert

Behind-the-scenes posts: *"Currently reading [book title] and thinking about how it applies to the work I do with clients around [theme]. Anyone else fascinated by [concept]?"*

Educational content with personality: *"Three things I wish more people knew about therapy: 1) It's not just for crisis, 2) You don't need to have everything figured out before you start, 3) The right therapist makes all the difference."*

Seasonal content: *"Fall energy hits different. Anyone else feeling that urge to organize everything and start new routines? Sometimes this time of year brings up anxiety about change, and that's completely normal."*

Values-based content: *"Reminder: You don't have to earn the right to take up space. You don't have to be perfect to deserve support. You don't have to have it all together to ask for help."*

Email Marketing for Therapists

Most therapists think email marketing isn't for them, but it's one of the most effective ways to stay connected with your referral network and potential clients.

Building Your List Authentically

Offer valuable resources: Create simple downloads like "5 Questions to Ask Yourself Before Starting Therapy" or "A Guide to Finding the Right Therapist for You."

Share your expertise: Send monthly emails with insights, resources, or reflections on themes you see in your practice.

Stay connected with referral sources: Quarterly updates to your professional network about your current availability and any new offerings.

My Email Strategy

I started with a simple monthly newsletter that combined practice updates with genuinely helpful content. I wasn't trying to sell anything; I was trying to be useful.

The result? When people were ready for therapy or

had someone to refer, I was top of mind because I'd been consistently showing up with value.

Boundary Language for Success

As your practice grows, you'll need language for common scenarios that maintain professionalism while protecting your boundaries.

When Your Schedule is Full

"Thank you so much for reaching out. I'm currently full with a waitlist, but I'd be happy to provide you with referrals to other excellent therapists who might be a good fit. I also offer [alternative options like groups or intensives] if you're interested in those options."

For Rate Shopping

"I understand that cost is an important consideration. My rate reflects my specialization, experience, and the value of private-pay therapy. I want to make sure you find the right fit both clinically and financially, so I'm happy to provide referrals to other qualified therapists if that would be helpful."

For Scope of Practice Issues

"That's not within my area of expertise, but I know some excellent therapists who specialize in exactly what you're looking for. I'd be happy to provide some referrals."

Making It All Work Together

The most effective messaging strategy is one where all your platforms and materials work together to tell a consistent story about who you are, who you serve, and what makes you different.

Your website speaks to your ideal client's late-night worries. Your consultation calls demonstrate your expertise and approach. Your social media shows your personality and values. Your email communications keep you top of mind. Your referral conversations clearly communicate your specialization.

When these pieces align, you create what I call "messaging momentum" - every interaction reinforces and amplifies the others.

What's Coming Next

In the next chapter, we're going to talk about the client

journey - from that first website visit through ongoing therapy. We'll cover prequalifying strategies that save you time and energy, consultation processes that feel authentic, and how to create an experience that keeps ideal clients engaged while naturally screening out those who aren't a good fit.

Because here's the thing: great messaging gets people in the door, but a great client experience keeps them there and turns them into your biggest referral sources.

"Your website should feel like a conversation with your ideal client, not a resume for a licensing board."

Chapter Action Steps:

✓ Audit your current website copy - does it speak to your ideal client?

✓ Write one piece of fall-themed content for your practice

✓ Practice your consultation call structure out loud

Chapter 4: The Client Journey

Creating an Experience, Not Just Sessions

One of the biggest shifts I made in building my private pay practice was thinking about the entire client experience, not just what happened in the therapy room. From the moment someone finds your website to the way you handle endings, every touchpoint shapes their perception of value and their likelihood to refer others.

This comprehensive approach to the client journey is what separates successful private pay practices from those that struggle to retain clients or generate referrals. It's not enough to be a good therapist anymore - you need to create an experience that clients value and remember.

In this chapter, we'll walk through each stage of the client journey, providing specific strategies to make each touchpoint intentional and effective.

Stage 1: Discovery and First Impression

Most potential clients will interact with your online presence before they ever speak with you. This means your website, social media, and online reviews are doing therapy work before you even meet.

The Pre-Contact Experience

Your Website as Your First Session: Think of your website as the first therapeutic intervention. It should help potential clients feel understood, normalize their struggles, and give them hope that change is possible.

Key Elements That Work:

- Clear, warm photos that show your personality
- Language that speaks to their internal experience, not just symptoms
- Easy ways to take the next step

What I Learned From Tracking My Website: When I started paying attention to my website analytics, I discovered that people were spending an average of 4-5 minutes reading my content before deciding whether to contact me. That's significant engagement, which told me they were considering whether I might be the right fit.

This insight transformed my approach to my website content. Instead of merely listing services, I began developing content that helped people understand what therapy with me would truly be like.

Stage 2: The Prequalifying Process

This is where most therapists miss a huge opportunity. Instead of hoping that anyone who calls will be a good fit, you can design a process that helps ideal clients self-select and others recognize they'd be better served elsewhere.

Why Prequalifying Matters

From my years of consultation work, I've seen therapists burn out from working with the wrong clients far more often than from working too much with the right clients. Prequalifying isn't about being elitist - it's about being efficient and effective.

Benefits of Prequalifying:

- *Reduces time spent on consultations that won't convert*

- *Increases client satisfaction and retention*

- *Positions you as a specialist rather than a generalist*

- *Reduces therapy dropouts and no-shows*

- *Creates better clinical outcomes*

The Prequalifying Framework

Key Indicators of an Ideal Client:

- *They understand and value your specialization*
- *They're financially prepared for private pay therapy*
- *They express clear goals and readiness to engage*
- *They've done some research about therapy and your approach*
- *They can commit to the time and consistency therapy requires*

Red Flags to Watch For:

- *Asking if you bill insurance when your website clearly states you don't*

- *Wanting a "quick fix" or unclear about therapy goals*

- *Rate shopping or trying to negotiate fees*
- *Unwillingness to commit to regular sessions*
- *Expecting you to solve problems they're not willing to work on*

Prequalifying Questions That Work

I developed these questions through years of consultation calls:

1. *"**What led you to seek therapy right now?**" This tells you about their motivation and timing.*

2. *"**Have you worked with a therapist before?**" Their previous therapy experience reveals a lot about their expectations and readiness.*

3. *"**What are your goals for therapy?**" Vague answers might indicate they're not ready for the work.*

4. *"**Are you familiar with how private pay therapy works?**" This assesses whether individuals understand the investment they're making.*

5. "**How do you plan to prioritize your time and financial investment in this work?"** *This assesses their commitment level.*

Case Study: Transforming the Consultation Process

Let me tell you about a talented therapist who was spending hours each week on consultation calls that rarely converted to actual clients. She was exhausted and starting to doubt her abilities.

The problem wasn't her clinical skills - it was her consultation process. She was taking calls from anyone who reached out, spending 30-45 minutes on each call, and often ending up with people who weren't ready for therapy or weren't a good fit for her approach.

Here's what we changed:

Before:

- *No screening process before consultation calls*
- *Long consultation calls with everyone who inquired*
- *Talking more than listening during consultations*
- *Not clearly explaining her approach or fees*

- *Hoping people would choose her rather than assessing mutual fit*

After:

- *Brief phone screening before scheduling consultation calls*
- *20-minute focused consultation structure*
- *Clear questions to assess readiness and fit*
- *Confident explanation of her approach and fees*
- *Mutual assessment rather than one-way sales pitch*

The Results:

- *Consultation-to-client conversion rate increased from 30% to 75%*
- *Time spent on consultations decreased by 60%*
- *Client retention improved significantly*
- *Her confidence in her process increased dramatically*

The key insight? She realized that the right clients prefer a straightforward, structured process. It helps them feel confident that they're making a good decision.

Stage 3: The Decision Point - Consultation vs. Direct Scheduling

Here's where therapists take different approaches, and both can work depending on your style and business model.

Option 1: The Consultation Call Approach

Some therapists use consultation calls as a way to assess mutual fit before scheduling. This can work well if you position it correctly and value your time appropriately.

Option 2: The Streamlined Approach (My Method)

I've found that if you're clear enough on your website about who you work with and how you work, you can eliminate the consultation call and move directly to scheduling intake appointments.

How I Handle Initial Contact:

Clear Website Information: I make sure my website answers the key prequalifying questions:

- Who I work with specifically
- What my approach involves
- What my fees are
- How the process works

- *What to expect*

Phone Calls: *If someone calls and I'm available, I'll answer quick questions - maybe 2-3 minutes maximum. I'm not opposed to being helpful, but I don't provide free consultations.*

Email Questions: *I'll answer a few brief questions via email, but I won't go back and forth in lengthy exchanges. If someone needs extensive information, that's what the intake session is for.*

Direct to Intake: *People schedule directly for an intake appointment where we do the real work of assessing fit and beginning therapy.*

Why This Works:

- *Respects both my time and theirs*
- *Attracts people who are ready to invest in the process*
- *Eliminates the "maybe" clients who want to shop around endlessly*
- *Creates clear boundaries from the first interaction*

My Philosophy on Free Work

I learned early in my private pay journey that when you give away your expertise for free, people often value it accordingly. By requiring an investment of my time and insight, I attract clients who are serious about the work and ready to engage meaningfully.

This doesn't mean being cold or unhelpful. It means being clear about the value of your time and expertise.

Stage 4: Onboarding and Early Sessions

How you handle the transition from consultation to the first session sets the tone for the entire therapeutic relationship.

The Onboarding Process That Works

Confirmation and Preparation: *Send a clear email confirming the first session with:*

- *Date, time, and location (or video platform details)*
- *What to expect in the first session*
- *Any paperwork they need to complete*
- *Your cancellation policy*
- *Payment information*

First Session Focus: *Instead of just gathering history, focus on:*

- *Reinforcing why they chose to start therapy now*
- *Clarifying their goals and expectations*
- *Explaining your approach in more detail*
- *Beginning to build therapeutic rapport*
- *Setting the framework for how you'll work together*

Setting Expectations: *Be clear about:*

- *How often you'll meet*
- *What they can expect from you*
- *What you need from them*
- *How you'll track progress*
- *What success looks like*

My First Session Evolution

I used to spend the first sessions entirely on intake paperwork and history-taking. Clients would leave feeling like they hadn't really started therapy yet.

Now I balance essential information-gathering with actually starting the therapeutic work. People leave the first session feeling like they've made a genuine step forward, not merely completed an assessment.

Stage 5: The Ongoing Therapeutic Experience

This is where your clinical skills shine, but there are business elements that support the therapeutic work and enhance the overall experience.

Creating Consistency and Value

Reliable Structure:

- *Consistent session times when possible*
- *Clear communication about schedule changes*
- *Professional but warm session environment*
- *Predictable session flow that feels therapeutic*

Demonstrating Value:

- *Regular check-ins about progress and goals*
- *Homework or between-session support when appropriate*
- *Flexibility in approach based on their evolving needs*
- *Clear connections between the work you're doing and their stated goals*

Building the Relationship:

- *Remembering details from previous sessions*
- *Celebrating progress and acknowledging challenges*
- *Being genuinely curious about their experience*
- *Maintaining appropriate boundaries while being authentically present*

Case Study: The Power of Intentional Experience

A genuinely compassionate and successful therapist was struggling with client retention. People would start strong but often drop out after a few months, even when they were making progress.

The issue wasn't his therapeutic skills - it was that the overall experience felt disjointed. Sessions were valuable, but there was no sense of journey or progression.

Monthly Progress Reviews: *Brief check-ins about what was working, what needed adjustment, and what they wanted to focus on next.*

Clear Session Structure: *Opening check-in, focused work, closing summary of insights, and next steps.*

Between-Session Connection: *Occasional emails with resources related to what they were working on (not therapy advice, just relevant articles or tools).*

Celebration of Progress: *Explicit acknowledgment of changes and growth, however small.*

The Results: *His client retention increased from an average of 3 months to over 8 months, and his referrals increased significantly because clients felt so supported throughout their experience.*

Stage 6: Transitions and Endings

How you handle transitions - whether planned endings, referrals to other providers, or unexpected changes - impacts not only the current client but your reputation and future referrals.

Ethical and Effective Endings

When Therapy Goals Are Met:

- *Acknowledge the progress made*
- *Reinforce their growth and capabilities*
- *Discuss maintenance of changes*

- *Leave the door open for future check-ins*
- *Ask for feedback about their experience*

When Referral is Needed:

- *Be honest about when someone needs a different expertise*
- *Provide specific, warm referrals*
- *Offer to communicate with the new provider (with permission)*
- *Frame the referral as continued care, not rejection*

When Clients Choose to End:

- *Respect their decision while offering to discuss concerns*
- *Provide a summary of progress made*
- *Offer resources for continued growth*

- *Maintain warmth and professionalism*

My Approach to Endings

I learned that how I handled endings affected not just that client, but often their family members, friends, and colleagues who might need therapy in the future. Good endings create referrals; difficult endings can damage your reputation.

I now approach every ending as an opportunity to reinforce the value of therapy and leave people with a positive association with getting help.

Creating Your Client Journey Map

Take some time to map out your current client journey:

1. **Discovery:** *How do people find you? What's their experience with your online presence?*

2. **Initial Contact:** *What happens when someone reaches out? How quickly do you respond? What information do you gather?*

3. **Consultation:** *How do you structure these calls? What questions do you ask? How do you explain your approach?*

4. **Onboarding:** *How do you transition from consultation to the first session? What preparation do you provide?*

5. **Ongoing Work:** *What does the therapeutic experience feel like? How do you track and celebrate progress?*

6. **Transitions:** *How do you handle endings, referrals, and changes in the therapeutic relationship?*

Questions for Reflection

- *Where in your current process do potential clients get confused or drop out?*
- *What touchpoints could you improve to demonstrate value better?*
- *How could you make the experience feel more intentional and cohesive?*
- *What feedback have you received about your process that you haven't acted on?*

What's Coming Next

In the next chapter, we're going to talk about networking and building the professional relationships that become your most significant source of referrals. We'll cover everything from authentic networking strategies to maintaining referral relationships over time.

Because here's the truth: while a great client experience keeps people engaged and creates some word-of-mouth referrals, a strong professional network creates consistent, high-quality referrals that can fill your practice with ideal clients.

"Creating an experience rather than just offering sessions is what transforms a practice from transactional to transformational."

Chapter Action Steps:

✓ Map out your current client journey from first contact to ending

✓ Identify one place where you can improve the client experience

✓ Create or update your consultation call script

✓ Design your ideal onboarding process

Chapter 5:
Networking That
Actually Works

Beyond the Business Cards

Let me be honest with you: networking used to make me feel gross. The whole idea of "working a room" and collecting business cards felt inauthentic and pushy. As someone who went into therapy to help people, not to sell things, the traditional approach to networking felt completely wrong.

But here's what I learned: networking for therapists isn't about sales. It's about building genuine professional relationships that create mutual value. When you approach networking from a place of curiosity and service rather than need and promotion, everything changes.

The therapists who struggle to build referral networks aren't necessarily less skilled clinically. They often just haven't learned how to build professional relationships systematically. This chapter will change that for you.

The Relationship-First Approach

After years of building my referral network and helping hundreds of other therapists do the same, I've discovered that the most successful networking happens when you focus on relationships first and referrals second.

My Networking Evolution

In my early days of private practice, I thought networking meant going to mental health association meetings and hoping people would remember me. I'd show up, exchange pleasantries, hand out business cards, and wonder why referrals weren't flowing in.

The shift occurred when I began approaching networking with genuine curiosity about other people's work, rather than hoping they'd send me clients. I started asking questions like:

- *"What population do you most enjoy working with?"*
- *"What's been most rewarding about your practice lately?"*
- *"What challenges are you seeing in your work?"*

Suddenly, conversations became interesting instead of awkward, and people started remembering me not as someone who wanted their referrals, but as someone who cared about their work.

The Foundation: Knowing Your Value Proposition

Before you can network effectively, you need to be crystal clear about who you serve and how you're different from other therapists. This isn't about being better - it's about being specific.

Your 30-Second Introduction

Practice completing this statement until it flows naturally: "I'm [name], a [credentials] who specializes in helping [specific population] with [specific challenge] so they can [specific outcome]."

For example: "I'm Sarah, a licensed professional counselor who specializes in helping women entrepreneurs manage perfectionism and burnout so they can build sustainable businesses without sacrificing their well-being."

This is infinitely more memorable than "I'm a therapist who works with anxiety and depression."

What Makes You Referable

Think about these questions:

- *What specific expertise do you have that other therapists might not?*
- *What types of clients do you genuinely enjoy working with?*
- *What approaches or techniques are you exceptionally skilled in?*
- *What personal or professional experiences inform your work?*

Your goal isn't to be everything to everyone. Your goal is to be the obvious choice for your specific area of expertise.

Building Your Referral Network Systematically

Random networking rarely produces consistent results. Successful referral networks are built systematically, with intention and follow-through.

Identifying Your Ideal Referral Sources

Direct Referral Sources (other therapists):

- *Therapists who don't work with your population*
- *Therapists with full practices who need overflow referrals*
- *Therapists with complementary specializations*
- *Therapists who only take insurance and need private pay referrals*

Indirect Referral Sources (non-therapists):

- *Primary care physicians*
- *Psychiatrists*
- *Life coaches*
- *Attorneys (family law, employment law)*
- *Employee assistance program coordinators*
- *Clergy*
- *Massage therapists*
- *Acupuncturists*

Professional Organizations and Groups:

- *Local mental health associations*
- *Professional specialty groups (trauma, addiction, etc.)*

- *Business networking groups*
- *Online professional communities*

The Systematic Approach

Month 1: Research and Planning

- *Identify 20 potential referral sources in your area*
- *Research their specializations and approaches*
- *Find natural connection points*

Month 2: Initial Outreach

- *Reach out to 5 people per week*
- *Suggest brief coffee meetings or phone calls*
- *Focus on learning about their work*

Month 3: Follow-Up and Relationship Building

- *Send thank you notes and resources to people you've met*
- *Make introductions between people in your network*
- *Begin referring to others when appropriate*

Ongoing: Maintenance and Growth

- *Quarterly check-ins with your network*
- *Regular addition of new contacts*
- *Consistent value-add communications*

Case Study: From Isolation to Integration

Let me tell you about another talented therapist who had been in solo practice for five years but was getting almost no referrals from other professionals. He was clinically excellent but professionally isolated.

His situation was common - he'd moved to a new city, hung out his shingle, and hoped people would find him. He was busy enough with online marketing, but he wanted more professional referrals and felt disconnected from the therapeutic community.

Here's how we systematically built his referral network:

Assessment Phase: *We identified that he specialized in working with men dealing with life transitions - divorce, career changes, midlife issues. This was an underserved population in his area.*

Strategic Planning: *We created a list of potential referral sources:*

- *Family law attorneys*
- *Divorce mediators*
- *Career counselors*

- *Employee assistance programs*
- *Primary care physicians in his area*
- *Therapists who primarily worked with women and children*

Systematic Outreach: *Tom committed to reaching out to 3 new professionals each week. His approach was simple: "Hi [Name], I'm Tom, a therapist who specializes in working with men going through major life transitions. I'd love to learn more about your work and see if there are ways we might support each other's clients. Would you be open to a brief coffee meeting?"*

Results After Six Months:
- *Built relationships with 15 professionals who regularly referred to him*
- *Became known as "the guy who works with men" in his professional community*
- *Increased referrals by 300%*
- *Felt professionally connected and supported*

The key insight? He stopped trying to be known by everyone and started focusing on being known by the right people for the right reasons.

The Art of Professional Conversations

Effective networking conversations have a structure, but they should feel natural and genuinely curious.

The Conversation Framework

Opening (Build Rapport): *"Thanks for taking the time to meet. I'm always interested in connecting with other professionals who serve [relevant population]. Tell me about your practice."*

Learning (Understand Their Work):

- *"What population do you most enjoy working with?"*
- *"What types of clients do you find most rewarding?"*
- *"What are the biggest challenges you're seeing in your work lately?"*
- *"What kinds of referrals are you looking for?"*

Sharing (Communicate Your Value): *"I specialize in [your area] and work primarily with [your population]. I find this work rewarding because [authentic reason]. I'm always looking to connect with professionals who work with [complementary populations] since we might be able to support each other's clients."*

Exploring Collaboration: *"Are there types of situations where you find yourself wishing you had someone to refer to who specialized in [your area]?" "What would be helpful for you to know about my practice?"*

Following Up: *"I'd love to stay connected. Would it be helpful if I sent you a brief overview of my specialization?" "I'll keep you in mind if I encounter clients who might benefit from your expertise."*

My Networking Breakthrough

I used to think networking was about convincing people to refer to me. The breakthrough came when I shifted to thinking about how I could be helpful to other professionals.
I began asking myself: "How can I make this person's work easier or better?" Sometimes that involved making referrals to them, sometimes sharing resources, and other times simply being a supportive professional colleague.

This shift changed everything. People started seeing me not as someone who wanted something from them, but as someone who added value to their professional lives.

Digital Networking That Works

While in-person networking is valuable, digital networking has become equally important, especially post-pandemic.

LinkedIn for Therapists

Optimizing Your Profile:

- *Professional photo that shows your personality*
- *Headline that clearly states your specialization*
- *Summary that speaks to your ideal referral sources*
- *Regular posts about your area of expertise*

Connection Strategy: *"Hi [Name], I enjoyed [where you met/what you have in common]. I'm a therapist specializing in [your niche] and would love to connect with other professionals in our field. Looking forward to staying in touch!"*

Content That Builds Relationships:

- *Insights about your specialization*
- *Professional observations (without violating confidentiality)*
- *Resources that might help other professionals*

- *Thoughtful commentary on industry trends*

Professional Facebook Groups

Many local areas have therapist Facebook groups that can be goldmines for networking.

How to Engage Effectively:
- *Introduce yourself thoughtfully when you join*
- *Answer questions in your area of expertise*
- *Share resources when appropriate*
- *Ask for advice when you need referrals for clients*

Sample Introduction: *"Hi everyone! I'm [Name], a [credentials] in [location] specializing in [niche]. I work privately with [ideal clients] and am always happy to connect with other professionals serving similar populations. Looking forward to learning from this community!"*

The Follow-Up System That Actually Works

Most networking fails not because of bad initial conversations, but because of a lack of follow-up.

My Follow-Up Framework

Within 24 Hours: *Send a brief thank you note: "Thanks for taking the time to chat today. I enjoyed learning about your work with [specific detail]. I'll keep you in mind for [relevant referrals]."*

Within One Week: *Send any resources you promised or relevant articles related to your conversation.*

Monthly Check-Ins: *Brief touch-base with your most promising connections. Not asking for anything, just staying connected.*

Quarterly Updates: *Send broader updates to your network about your current availability, any new services, or changes in your practice.*

Template: Professional Follow-Up

Subject: *Following up on our connection*

Hi [Name],

Thanks for taking the time to connect with me yesterday. I appreciate you sharing insights about your practice and client population.

I wanted to follow up with [specific thing you offered - resource, contact, etc.].

I'm here as a resource anytime you have clients who might benefit from [your specialization]. I'll also keep you in mind for [what they do].

Looking forward to staying connected!

[Your name]

Creating Mutual Value

The best referral relationships are built on mutual benefit, not one-way requests.

Ways to Add Value to Your Network

Make Introductions: *Connect people in your network who might benefit from knowing each other.*

Share Resources: *Send articles, books, or tools that might be useful to specific people in your network.*

Offer Consultation: *Be available for brief, informal consultations about cases in your area of expertise.*

Provide Feedback: *Offer to review websites, marketing materials, or other professional content.*

Share Opportunities: *Let people know about speaking opportunities, training programs, or professional openings.*

Case Study: The Power of Giving First

A fellow Southern therapist was frustrated because she felt like she was always asking for referrals but rarely receiving them. The problem was that she hadn't established herself as someone who gave value first.

We shifted her approach:
- *She started a monthly email newsletter with resources for other professionals*
- *She began making introductions between people in her network*
- *She offered to present on her specialization at local professional groups*
- *She became known for having great referral sources for various specializations*

The Result: *Within six months, she became a central hub in her professional community. People started referring to her not just because she was good at what she did, but because she was someone who made everyone's professional life better.*

Tracking Your Network

You can't manage what you don't measure. Keep track of your networking efforts systematically.

Simple Tracking Categories

Hot Leads: *Active referral sources who send regularly*

Warm Connections: *Professional relationships to nurture*

Cold Prospects: *New contacts to follow up with*

Collaborators: *Potential partners for groups, workshops, or other projects*

Information to Track

- *Contact information*
- *Specialization and ideal clients*
- *When you last connected*
- *Referrals sent (both directions)*

- *Personal details that help you connect*
- *Follow-up reminders*

My Tracking Evolution

I started with a simple spreadsheet and eventually moved to a basic CRM system. The key isn't having fancy technology - it's having a system you'll actually use consistently.

The professionals who succeed at networking are those who treat relationship-building as systematically as they treat their clinical work.

Common Networking Mistakes to Avoid

Mistake 1: Only Networking When You Need Something
Build relationships consistently, not just when your practice is slow.

Mistake 2: Focusing Only on Other Therapists *Some of your best referral sources might be non-therapists who work with your ideal population.*

Mistake 3: Being Too Generic *"I work with anxiety and depression" is forgettable. "I help high-achieving women with perfectionism" is memorable.*

*Mistake 4: **Not Following Up*** *Most networking happens in the follow-up, not the initial meeting.*

*Mistake 5: **Making It All About You*** *Focus on being interested, not just interesting.*

Building Your Networking Plan

Week 1: Assessment

- *List your current professional relationships*
- *Identify gaps in your referral network*
- *Research potential networking opportunities in your area*

Week 2: Planning

- *Choose 2-3 networking activities to focus on*
- *Develop your 30-second introduction*
- *Set up your tracking system*

Week 3: Action

- *Reach out to 5 potential connections*
- *Attend one networking event*
- *Follow up with recent contacts*

Week 4: Evaluation

- Assess what's working and what isn't
- Adjust your approach based on results
- Plan for the following month

What's Coming Next

In the next chapter, we'll explore innovative service delivery options to help you scale your impact and income beyond traditional 50-minute sessions. We'll cover therapy intensives, group offerings, and other creative approaches that many private pay practitioners are using successfully.

These alternative service delivery models can help you serve more people, create more flexibility in your schedule, and generate additional revenue streams while still maintaining the high-touch, personalized approach that makes private pay therapy so valuable.

"Your next referral might come from someone you haven't even met yet. Networking doesn't have to be sleazy or awkward. Done right, it's simply a human connection with purpose."

Chapter Action Steps:

✓ List 10 potential referral partners in your area
✓ Reach out to 2 colleagues for coffee chats this month
✓ Attend one networking event (online or in-person)
✓ Send one thoughtful follow-up message from a recent connection

Chapter 6: Innovative Service Delivery

Beyond the 50-Minute Hour

One of the most significant advantages of private pay practice is the freedom to design services that serve your clients' needs rather than insurance company requirements. While the traditional 50-minute weekly session works well for many clients, it's not the only way to deliver effective therapy.

In this chapter, we're going to explore alternative service delivery models that can help you serve more people, create more flexibility in your schedule, and generate additional revenue streams. These aren't gimmicks or ways to shortcut the therapeutic process - they're legitimate approaches that often create better outcomes than traditional therapy alone.

I've personally used several of these models in my practice, and I've consulted with hundreds of therapists who have successfully implemented them. The key is choosing approaches that align with your clinical expertise and your clients' needs.

Therapy Intensives: Deep Work in Condensed Time

Therapy intensives are extended, focused sessions that allow clients to make significant progress in a compressed timeframe. Instead of spreading work across months of weekly sessions, you create concentrated experiences that can accelerate healing and insight.

Why Intensives Work

For Clients:

- *Faster progress on specific issues*
- *Ability to go deeper without weekly interruptions*
- *Better for busy schedules or travel constraints*
- *Intensive focus can break through stuck patterns*
- *Clear beginning and end creates commitment*

For Therapists:

- *Higher income per day worked*
- *Fewer total client contact hours for equivalent income*
- *Deeper, more satisfying clinical work*
- *Attracts motivated, invested clients*
- *Creates schedule flexibility*

Types of Intensives I've Used

Half-Day Deep Dive (4 hours): Perfect for working through specific traumas, relationship issues, or major life decisions. Structure includes breaks and different therapeutic activities.

Full-Day Intensive (6-8 hours): Comprehensive work on complex issues. Might include individual sessions, journaling time, movement or mindfulness practices, and integration planning.

Weekend Retreats (2-3 days): For major life transitions, intensive trauma work, or comprehensive relationship therapy. Can be done individually or with couples.

Multi-Session Packages: A combination of intensive sessions and follow-up appointments over a defined period.

My Experience with Intensives

I've occasionally experimented with intensives when specific situations called for them. For example, a client was moving across the country and wanted to complete *as much work as possible before leaving, so we scheduled a 6-hour session. The depth of work we achieved was remarkable.*

That experience taught me that some therapeutic work can benefit from sustained focus rather than being divided into weekly segments. While intensives aren't a regular part of my practice, I offer them selectively when they address specific client needs and situations.

Structuring an Effective Intensive

Pre-Intensive Preparation:

- *Clear intake process to assess appropriateness*
- *Specific goals and expectations setting*
- *Pre-work assignments or reflection questions*
- *Logistics planning (location, breaks, materials)*

Sample Full-Day Structure:

- **9:00-10:30:** *Opening session and goal setting*
- **10:30-10:45:** *Break*
- **10:45-12:15:** *Deep therapeutic work*
- **12:15-1:15:** *Lunch break*
- **1:15-2:45:** *Continued therapeutic work*
- **2:45-3:00:** *Break*

- *3:00-4:30:* Integration and planning
- *4:30-5:00:* Closing and next steps

Post-Intensive Support:

- Follow-up session within 1-2 weeks
- Check-in calls or emails
- Resource recommendations
- Integration support

Pricing Intensives

Don't price intensives by multiplying your hourly rate. Price them based on the transformation and value provided. Consider:

- The concentrated expertise and attention
- The accelerated progress is possible
- The convenience and efficiency for the client
- Your preparation and follow-up time
- The intensive nature of the work

Typical ranges I see: $750-$2,500+, depending on length, specialization, and market.

Group Therapy: Scaling Your Impact

Group therapy enables you to serve a larger number of people while creating powerful healing experiences that individual therapy can't replicate. The key is designing groups that attract your ideal clients and deliver real value.

Why Groups Work in Private Pay

Clinical Benefits:

- *Peer support and shared experience*
- *Opportunity to practice new skills with others*
- *Reduced isolation and shame*
- *Different perspectives on similar issues*
- *Cost-effective way to access specialized treatment*

Business Benefits:

- *Higher income per hour worked*
- *Ability to serve more people with specialized expertise*
- *Creates community around your practice*
- *Attracts people who want both individual and group work*
- *Can be more sustainable than only seeing individuals*

My Group Therapy Success

When I first considered offering groups, I was nervous about whether people would sign up. The solution started with a clear, specific focus rather than a generic therapy group.

My first group was for codependency - something I could speak to both professionally and personally. It was consistently full, and we had templates and materials that sustained us for a full year. The group ran smoothly because I had a clear structure and knew the content deeply.

I made the mistake later of trying to cram similar content into shorter sessions, which I didn't like at all. I had a formula that worked, and when I changed it, both the group and I suffered.

Now my groups are solely focused on sex addiction recovery, and I only offer two-hour sessions that are open-ended with a maximum of six members. Codependency is part of the modules I teach, along with trauma work. This structure allows for the depth of work that these complex issues require while maintaining the intimate, safe environment that makes group therapy effective for this population.

Designing Successful Groups

Clear Population Focus:

- Women entrepreneurs dealing with perfectionism
- Men navigating divorce and life transitions
- Healthcare workers managing burnout
- Parents of teens with anxiety
- Professionals in specific recovery situations

Structured Format:

- Defined duration (8 weeks, 12 weeks, ongoing)
- Consistent meeting time and location
- Clear group guidelines and expectations
- Mix of psychoeducation and process work
- Homework or between-session activities

Size and Logistics:

- Ideal size: 6-8 members for therapy groups
- Open vs. closed enrollment
- Virtual or in-person
- Fee structure (per session, package deal, monthly)

Group Launch Strategy

8 Weeks Before Launch:

- *Define group focus and structure*
- *Create marketing materials*
- *Update website with group information*
- *Plan intake/screening process*

4 Weeks Before Launch:

- *Begin marketing and outreach*
- *Start accepting applications*
- *Schedule intake calls with interested participants*
- *Prepare group materials and space*

Launch Week:

- *Confirm all participants*
- *Send welcome information and logistics*
- *Prepare for first session*
- *Set up tracking systems for attendance and progress*

Case Study: From Idea to Success

A consultee wanted to start a group for women dealing with anxiety, but her first attempt struggled because it was too generic. We worked together to narrow the focus to "high-achieving women who struggle with perfectionism and people-pleasing."

The refined approach was completely different:

- Clear marketing message that spoke to specific struggles
- Pre-group workshop to introduce concepts and build interest
- Specific 10-week curriculum focused on perfectionism
- Higher fee that attracted committed participants
- Full enrollment within two weeks of announcement

The key insight? Specificity creates demand. Generic groups struggle to fill; specific groups create their own market.

Session Packages and Retainers

Instead of session-by-session payment, some therapists offer packages that create commitment and predictable revenue.

Package Structures That Work

Problem-Focused Packages:

- "Anxiety Breakthrough" - 8 sessions

focused on anxiety management

- *"Relationship Reset" - 6 sessions for couples in transition*

- *"Life Transition Support" - 10 sessions for major life changes*

Time-Based Packages:

- *3-month intensive support package*
- *6-month comprehensive therapy program*
- *Annual retainer for ongoing support*

Hybrid Packages:

- *Combination of individual sessions, group participation, and email support*
- *Intensive session plus follow-up appointments*
- *Therapy plus coaching for specific goals*

Benefits of Package Approaches

For Clients:

- *Clear expectations about duration and cost*
- *Reduced decision fatigue about continuing*
- *Often better value than session-by-session*

- *Encourages commitment to the process*

For Therapists:

- *Predictable revenue*
- *Reduced administrative overhead*
- *Attracts committed clients*
- *Allows for comprehensive treatment planning*

Virtual Service Delivery

The pandemic accelerated the adoption of virtual therapy, but many therapists haven't fully explored the possibilities beyond introductory video sessions.

Innovative Virtual Approaches

Virtual Intensives:

- *Full-day virtual retreats with breaks and activities*
- *Walking therapy sessions via phone*
- *Virtual EMDR or other specialized treatments*

Asynchronous Support:

- *Voice message exchanges between sessions*
- *Video diary assignments with therapist feedback*

- *Secure messaging for check-ins and support*

Virtual Groups:

- *Online support groups with specialized focuses*
- *Virtual workshops and psychoeducational sessions*
- *Hybrid individual/group approaches*

My Virtual Evolution

Initially, I was skeptical about virtual therapy, thinking it would be less effective than in-person work. What I discovered was that for many clients, virtual sessions work better - they're more comfortable in their own space, more likely to be vulnerable, and appreciate the convenience.

I now offer virtual intensives that include movement breaks, journaling time, and creative exercises that wouldn't be possible in a traditional office setting.

Maintenance and Check-In Models

Not every client requires weekly therapy indefinitely. Establishing structures for ongoing support without intensive therapy can benefit clients while ensuring sustainable revenue.

Maintenance Session Structures

Monthly Check-Ins:

- *For clients who've completed intensive work*
- *Focus on maintaining progress and preventing relapse*
- *Lower fee structure than regular therapy*
- *Clear agenda and goals for each session*

Quarterly Reviews:

- *Comprehensive assessment of progress and goals*
- *Planning for upcoming challenges or opportunities*
- *Adjustment of strategies and skills*
- *Connection point for returning to regular therapy if needed*

As-Needed Support:

- *Retainer model for crisis or decision support*
- *Single sessions for specific issues*
- *Brief consultation for life decisions*

Pricing Alternative Service Models

Pricing these models requires thinking beyond hourly rates to value-based pricing.

Factors to Consider

Time Investment:

- Actual contact time
- Preparation time
- Follow-up requirements
- Administrative overhead

Expertise Required:

- Specialized training needed
- Years of experience
- Unique skills or approaches
- Risk and responsibility involved

Client Value:

- Convenience and flexibility
- Accelerated progress
- Comprehensive support
- Unique outcomes possible

Market Positioning:

- Premium vs. accessible pricing
- Competition in your area
- Target demographic

- *Perceived value in your market*

My Pricing Philosophy

I price based on transformation, not time. A 6-hour intensive that helps someone break through a pattern they've been stuck in for years is worth far more than six individual sessions spread over six weeks.

This doesn't mean overcharging, but it means recognizing that concentrated expertise and accelerated outcomes have premium value.

Implementation Strategy

Start Small and Test

Choose One Model: *Pick the alternative service delivery model that most excites you and aligns with your expertise.*

Test with Existing Clients: *Offer the new model to current clients who might benefit before marketing it broadly.*

Gather Feedback: *Get detailed feedback about the experience and outcomes to refine your approach.*

Refine and Scale: *Adjust based on what you learn, then begin marketing to new clients.*

Common Implementation Mistakes

Mistake 1: Offering Too Many Options *Start with one alternative model and master it before adding others.*

Mistake 2: Underpricing *Don't price alternative models as if they're just regular sessions bundled together.*

Mistake 3: Poor Boundaries *These models require even clearer boundaries than traditional therapy.*

Mistake 4: Inadequate Preparation *Alternative models often require more upfront planning than regular sessions.*

What's Coming Next

In the next chapter, we'll explore how to develop the CEO mindset and time management skills necessary to run your practice like a business. We'll cover everything from strategic thinking to managing the isolation that can come with solo practice.

Because here's the truth: clinical skills make you a good

therapist, but business skills make you a successful practice owner. The therapists who thrive in private pay aren't necessarily the most clinically gifted - they're the ones who understand how to build sustainable systems around their clinical work.

Chapter Action Steps:

✓ Choose ONE alternative service model that excites you
✓ Test the concept with one current client
✓ Research pricing for similar services in your market
✓ Create a simple outline for your new service offering

Chapter 7: CEO Mindset & Time Management

From Therapist to Business Owner

One of the biggest challenges I faced in transitioning to private pay wasn't clinical - it was mental. I had to shift from thinking like an employee who shows up and does therapy to thinking like a CEO who runs a business that happens to provide therapy services.

This mindset shift is crucial because, in private practice, you're not just a therapist. You're the CEO, marketing director, financial manager, administrative coordinator, and facilities manager of your business. The therapists who struggle aren't usually lacking clinical skills - they're lacking business skills and strategic thinking.

This chapter will help you develop the CEO mindset that allows you to work on your practice, not just in it, and create the time management systems that prevent burnout while building sustainable success.

The Transition from Community Mental Health

Let me share my journey because I think it illustrates the mental shifts required. When I moved from community mental health to private practice, I went through several stages.

Stage 1: Shared Office Space I rented space in a building with other therapists. We shared rooms and swapped spaces between sessions. It felt like a community mental health setting, but everyone had their own business. I still had some of that peer support and interaction, which was helpful during the transition.

Stage 2: Scaling Too Fast. After leaving the shared office space, I scaled quickly by offering leased space to other therapists and hiring staff. However, I became overwhelmed with administrative work, and the reduced clinical workload felt unfulfilling. Plus, I started taking insurance, and when payments were delayed, people still had to get paid, which meant I often went unpaid.

Stage 3: Downsizing and Learning I ended up downsizing, working from home for a bit, then moving to a solo office before finally transitioning to private pay. This experience taught me that bigger isn't always better, and that sustainable growth means maintaining what you love about the work.

Stage 4: Solo Practice and Isolation *In solo practice, I had to take extra effort to stay connected to people. I wasn't getting that casual peer feedback from running into colleagues in the hallway. The isolation hit me hard.*

Stage 5: CEO Mindset *The real breakthrough came when I stopped thinking of myself as "a therapist who happens to have a business" and started thinking of myself as "a business owner who provides therapy services." This shift changed everything about how I approached my work - and helped me understand that I could be successful without the complexity I'd tried before.*

Managing Loneliness in Solo Practice

Let's address this head-on because it's one of the biggest challenges in private practice that nobody talks about enough.

When Loneliness Shows Up

Loneliness in solo practice can manifest as:

- *Feeling like no one understands your business model or values*
- *Missing the peer consultation that happens naturally in group settings*
- *Exhaustion at the thought of reaching out for support*
- *Wondering "who do I call?" when you need professional guidance*
- *Feeling isolated from the broader therapeutic community*

My Strategies for Connection

When loneliness hits me, I have a plan:

- *Sometimes I take a nap (yes, really - self-care first)*
- *I get out of the house if I'm working from home - go for a drive, see a movie, change environments*
- *Once I've taken care of myself, I can send out texts asking "who's available to talk?"*
- *I maintain membership in consultation groups specifically for this support*

The key insight: I learned to go inside first, take care of myself and all my little parts, and then ask for what I need. It's easier to reach out when you're coming from a centered place rather than desperation.

Building Professional Support Systems

Formal Support:

- Regular consultation groups
- Professional associations and meetings
- Online therapist communities
- Peer supervision arrangements

Informal Support:

- Coffee meetings with other therapists
- Professional lunch groups
- Texting networks for quick check-ins
- Virtual co-working sessions

Strategic vs. Reactive Thinking

The biggest difference between therapists who struggle in private practice and those who thrive is their approach to business decisions.

Reactive Thinking (What I Used to Do)

- Accepting any client who calls
- Saying yes to every opportunity

- *Making decisions based on immediate financial pressure*
- *Responding to problems instead of preventing them*
- *Working harder instead of working smarter*

Strategic Thinking (What Changed Everything)

- *Being selective about clients to ensure a good fit*
- *Evaluating opportunities against long-term goals*
- *Making decisions based on overall practice vision*
- *Building systems to prevent problems*
- *Working systematically toward defined outcomes*

My Strategic Planning Process

Quarterly Reviews: *Every three months, I assess what's working, what isn't, and what needs to change.*

Annual Planning: *Once a year, I set significant goals and create action plans for achieving them.*

Monthly Check-ins: *Regular evaluation of progress toward goals and adjustment of strategies.*

Weekly Planning: *Every week, I identify the most critical business tasks and block time for them.*

Time Blocking for Practice Owners

This was a game-changer for me. Instead of letting my schedule happen to me, I started designing it intentionally.

The CEO Time Blocker Framework

The key is finding what works for your energy and your life. *Since I work primarily in the evenings with clients, my schedule looks different from therapists who see clients during traditional business hours.*

Morning Block (High Energy Time):

- *Strategic planning and big-picture thinking*
- *Content creation and marketing*
- *Financial reviews and business analysis*
- *System improvements and problem-solving*

Afternoon Block (Continued CEO Work):

- *Email and communication*
- *Networking activities*
- *Professional development*
- *Administrative tasks*

Evening Block (Client Sessions):

- *Scheduled client appointments*
- *Intake sessions*
- *Clinical documentation*

The framework is entirely flexible - *the point is to match your energy to the type of work you're doing. Some therapists do CEO work in the afternoon, others prefer mornings. Some see clients midday, while others see them in the evenings. Find what works for your natural rhythms and life circumstances.*

My Weekly Template

Monday: *Business planning and administrative tasks*

Tuesday-Thursday: *Primary client sessions (evenings)*

Wednesday: *Also consultation group meeting*

Friday: *Marketing, networking, and professional development*

This structure works for me, but yours might look completely different. *The goal is to create intentional blocks of time for different types of work*

*rather than trying to multitask constantly. Some
therapists prefer seeing clients in the morning, others
like afternoon or evening schedules. Design your
blocks around when you do your best work.*

The Power of Batching

*Instead of doing a little bit of everything every day, I
batch similar activities:*

*Content Creation: One morning per week for all social
media posts, blog articles, and newsletters*

*Financial Tasks: Monthly money dates for all financial
review and planning*

*Networking: Dedicated time blocks for outreach and
relationship building*

*Administrative: Specific times for scheduling, email,
and paperwork*

Financial Management for Therapists

*Most therapists hate talking about money, but
financial management is a core CEO
responsibility.*

My Financial Framework

Weekly Money Check:

- *Review weekly income and expenses*
- *Check cash flow and upcoming needs*
- *Identify any financial issues early*

Monthly Money Date:

- *Comprehensive financial review*
- *Update financial goals and projections*
- *Plan for upcoming expenses*
- *Celebrate financial wins*

Quarterly Financial Planning:

- *Assess progress toward annual financial goals*
- *Adjust pricing or services if needed*
- *Plan for seasonal fluctuations*
- *Review and adjust business strategy*

Annual Financial Review:

- *Complete financial analysis of the year*
- *Set financial goals for the coming year*
- *Plan significant investments or changes*

- *Update insurance and business protections*

Key Financial Metrics to Track

Revenue Metrics:

- *Monthly gross income*
- *Average income per client*
- *Number of sessions per month*
- *Seasonal patterns and trends*

Expense Metrics:

- *Fixed monthly expenses*
- *Variable costs per client*
- *Professional development investments*
- *Marketing and networking costs*

Profitability Metrics:

- *Net income after all expenses*
- *Profit margin percentage*
- *Cash flow patterns*
- *Financial runway (how long you could operate without income)*

Systems That Create Freedom

The goal of sound systems isn't to constrain you - it's to create freedom by handling routine decisions automatically.

Client Management Systems

Scheduling System:

- *Online scheduling that handles basics automatically*
- *Clear cancellation and rescheduling policies*
- *Automated reminders and confirmations*
- *Waitlist management for popular times*

Payment System:

- *Consistent payment collection method*
- *Clear financial policies*
- *Automatic superbill generation*

- *Outstanding balance tracking*

Communication System:

- *Standard email templates for everyday situations*
- *Clear boundaries around communication timing*
- *Consistent voice mail and email response times*

- *Emergency contact protocols*

Marketing Systems

Content Creation:

- *Editorial calendar for consistent posting*
- *Template library for common content types*
- *Batch creation and scheduling processes*
- *Performance tracking and optimization*

Networking Follow-up:

- *Contact management system*
- *Follow-up reminders and templates*
- *Referral tracking and acknowledgment*
- *Relationship maintenance scheduling*

My System Evolution

I started with basic systems and gradually sophisticated them as my practice grew. The key was implementing one system at a time and ensuring each one worked before adding complexity.

Now my systems handle most routine decisions automatically, which frees up my mental energy for strategic thinking and clinical work.

Managing Multiple Roles

As a solo practitioner, you wear many hats. The key is being intentional about when you're wearing which hat.

The Different Roles

Clinician: *Providing therapy services*

CEO: *Strategic planning and business development*

Marketing Director: *Creating and implementing marketing strategies*

Financial Manager: *Managing money and financial planning*

Administrator: *Handling scheduling, paperwork, and operations*

Professional: *Continuing education and professional development*

Role-Switching Strategies

Physical Transitions:

- Different spaces for different roles when possible
- Clothing changes to mark role transitions
- Specific materials and setups for each role

Mental Transitions:

- Brief rituals to shift between roles
- Clear time boundaries for each role
- Separate to-do lists for different functions

Temporal Boundaries:

- Specific days or times for each role
- Protected time for CEO work
- Clear "off limits" times for business tasks

Energy Management

Managing your energy is more important than managing your time because you can be efficient with your time, but if your energy is depleted, your effectiveness suffers.

Understanding Your Energy Patterns

Daily Energy Rhythms:

- When are you most creative and strategic?
- When do you have the most patience for clients?
- When is administrative work easiest?
- When do you need breaks and restoration?

Weekly Energy Patterns:

- Which days feel most energizing?
- When do you need lighter schedules?
- How does your energy change throughout the week?
- What pattern creates the most sustainability?

Seasonal Energy Patterns:

- How does your energy change with the seasons?
- When do you feel most motivated for growth?
- When do you need more restoration time?
- How can you plan around natural rhythms?

My Energy Management Strategy

I've learned that I have the most strategic thinking energy in the morning, so that's when I do CEO work. I *save client sessions for when I'm most present and patient. Administrative tasks get done when my energy is lower, but I still need to be productive.*

I also learned that I need buffer time between sessions and that back-to-back sessions all day drain me more than spreading them out with breaks.

Building Resilience for the Long Term

Private practice is a marathon, not a sprint. Building practices that sustain you over decades requires intentional resilience planning.

Preventing Burnout

Diversified Income: *Not putting all your eggs in the individual therapy basket - having groups, intensives, or other revenue streams.*

Flexible Schedule: *Building in time for vacation, sick days, and unexpected life events.*

Professional Development: *Continuing to grow and learn to prevent stagnation.*

Personal Support: Maintaining your own therapy, friendships, and life outside work.

Sustainable Growth Strategies

Gradual Expansion: Growing at a pace that doesn't overwhelm your systems or energy.

Quality over Quantity: Focusing on serving fewer people well rather than trying to help everyone.

Regular Evaluation: Consistently assessing what's working and what needs to change.

Flexibility: Being willing to adjust course when circumstances change.

What's Coming Next

In the next chapter, we'll discuss client retention and ethical offboarding, exploring when to continue working with someone and when to help them transition to something different. We'll also cover how to handle endings in ways that create positive referrals and maintain professional relationships.

Chapter Action Steps:

✓ Block out specific "CEO time" in your weekly schedule
✓ Identify your biggest time waster and create a boundary around it
✓ Set up one business system (scheduling, invoicing, or client management)
✓ Calculate your actual hourly rate, including all unpaid business tasks

Chapter 8: Client Retention & Ethical Offboarding

The Art of Knowing When to Stay and When to Go

One of the most challenging aspects of private practice is knowing when to continue working with a client and when to help them transition to something different. This isn't just a clinical decision - it's a business decision that affects your practice sustainability, your professional reputation, and ultimately your ability to serve other clients well.

In this chapter, we're going to explore how to make these decisions ethically and effectively, how to handle transitions gracefully, and how to turn endings into opportunities for future referrals and professional growth.

Understanding Retention vs. Offboarding

Healthy private practices balance retaining great-fit clients with ethically offboarding those who have met their goals or need different care. Both protect your well-being and your practice's sustainability.

The Retention Decision Framework

Is the client aligned with your niche and expertise? *If yes → Proceed with retention strategies; If no → Consider whether offboarding might serve them better*

Is progress continuing toward their goals? *If yes → Explore extending or deepening the work; If no → Reassess barriers, consider consultation, or evaluate fit*

Are sessions clinically productive and safe? *If yes → Retain and plan next phases of work; If no → Consider referring to someone with different expertise*

Has the client reached their goals or plateaued meaningfully? *If goals are met → Start conversations about next steps together If plateaued*

→ *Collaboratively evaluate whether continued work serves them*

When Retention Makes Sense

Indicators for Continuing Work

Strong Therapeutic Alliance:

- *Client feels heard and understood*
- *Trust and rapport are well-established*
- *Client is engaged and invested in the process*
- *Communication feels open and honest*

Ongoing Progress:

- *Movement toward stated goals, even if gradual*
- *Increased self-awareness and insight*
- *Development of new skills and coping strategies*
- *Positive changes in relationships or functioning*

Complex Issues Requiring Time:

- *Trauma work that needs sustained attention*
- *Deeply ingrained patterns that take time to shift*
- *Multiple interconnected issues requiring comprehensive*

approach

- *Preparation for major life transitions*

Client Expresses Desire to Continue:

- *Feels the work is valuable and beneficial*
- *Has specific goals for continued therapy*
- *Recognizes ongoing areas for growth*
- *Values the relationship and process*

Retention Strategies That Work

Regular Progress Reviews: *Schedule monthly or quarterly check-ins specifically to discuss:*

- *Progress toward goals*
- *What's working well in the therapy*
- *What might need adjustment*
- *New goals or areas to explore*

Goal Evolution: *Help clients recognize when initial goals have been met and support them in identifying new areas for growth:*

- *"We've made significant progress on your anxiety. What other areas of your life would you like to focus on?"*

- *"You've developed really strong communication skills. Are there other relationships where you'd like to practice these?"*

Celebrating Achievements: *Explicitly acknowledge progress and growth:*

- *"I want to take a moment to recognize how far you've come since we started."*

- *"The way you handled that situation shows real growth in your ability to set boundaries."*

Transparent Communication: *Be open about your assessment of their progress and the value of continued work:*

- *"I think there's still valuable work we could do together around..."*
- *"I'm wondering if you're feeling like this work is still serving you."*

When Offboarding Serves Everyone Better

Indicators for Ethical Offboarding

Goals Have Been Achieved:

- *Client has reached their stated objectives*
- *Symptoms have significantly improved*
- *Life functioning has stabilized*
- *Skills have been developed and integrated*

Plateau Without Progress:

- *Multiple sessions without meaningful movement*
- *Client seems to be maintaining rather than growing*
- *Lack of engagement or investment in the process*
- *Repetitive sessions without new insights*

Scope of Practice Issues:

- *Client needs expertise you don't have*
- *Issues have evolved beyond your training*
- *Specialized treatment would serve them better*
- *Medical or psychiatric needs require a different provider*

Poor Therapeutic Fit:

- *Personality or style mismatch that can't be resolved*
- *Different values or approaches to change*

- *Client would benefit from a different therapeutic approach*
- *Lack of rapport despite reasonable faith efforts*

Client Ambivalence or Resistance:

- *Consistently missing sessions or coming late*
- *Not engaging with the therapeutic process*
- *Expressing doubt about the value of therapy*
- *Going through the motions without investment*

My Philosophy on Endings

I learned early in my recovery journey, and later in my therapeutic practice, that how you handle endings matters enormously. In recovery, we talk about "good" endings versus "bad" endings - and the same principle applies in therapy.

A good ending leaves people with positive associations with getting help, confidence in their growth, and openness to seeking support in the future. A bad ending can create negative associations that prevent someone from getting help when they need it later.

I now approach every ending as an opportunity to reinforce the value of therapy and leave people with a sense of accomplishment and hope.

The Offboarding Conversation

Timing the Conversation

When You Recognize the Need: *Don't wait months hoping things will improve. If you're consistently questioning whether therapy is serving someone, it's time to have the conversation.*

When a client expresses ambivalence, such as saying "I'm not sure this is helping" or "Maybe I should take a break," it's best to *explore this openly rather than trying to convince them to stay.*

During Natural Transition Points: *Use goal achievements, life changes, or seasonal breaks as opportunities to reassess and discuss next steps.*

The Conversation Framework

Acknowledge the Relationship: *"I've really valued our work together and the progress you've made."*

State Your Observation: *"I've been reflecting on our*

recent sessions, and I'm wondering if we've accomplished what we set out to do when we started."

Invite Their Perspective: *"How are you feeling about the work we're doing? What's your sense of where you are in this process?"*

Explore Options Together: *"I see a few different directions we could go from here..."*

Support Their Decision: *"Whatever feels right to you, I want to support that decision."*

Sample Offboarding Scripts

- **When Goals Have Been Met:** *"Looking at where you were when we started and where you are now, you've made tremendous progress. You're handling your anxiety so differently, your relationships have improved, and you seem much more confident in yourself. I'm wondering if you're feeling ready to try things on your own for a while, knowing you can always come back if you need support."*

- **When Different Expertise is Needed:** *"As we've been working together, it's become clear that your struggles with eating have become central to what you're dealing* with. I think you'd be best served by someone who specializes specifically in eating disorders. I have some excellent referrals I'd like to share with you."

- **When Therapy Has Plateaued:** *"I've been noticing that our sessions feel different lately - more like check-ins than active therapy work. That might mean you're in a good place and don't need weekly therapy right now. What's your sense of that?"*

Case Study: A Graceful Ending

Let me tell you about my work with a client who came to me struggling with anxiety and work stress. We worked together for about eight months, and she made significant progress - her anxiety was manageable, she'd set better boundaries at work, and her relationships had improved. But our sessions started feeling routine. She was maintaining her progress but not growing, and I could sense some ambivalence about continuing.

How I Handled It: Instead of just continuing because she was paying and showing up, I brought up my observations: "I've been reflecting on our work together, and I'm struck by how much you've grown. When you first came in, you were having panic attacks regularly and feeling completely overwhelmed at work. Now you're managing your anxiety, you've set boundaries with your boss, and you seem so much more confident. I'm wondering how you're feeling about where we are in this process."

She admitted she'd been wondering the same thing but didn't know how to bring it up.

The Outcome: We spent two more sessions reviewing her progress, creating a plan for maintaining her gains, and discussing when she might want to return to therapy in the future. She left feeling accomplished and empowered.

Six months later, she referred a colleague to me, and a year later, she came back for a few sessions when she was going through a job transition. The ending had been so positive that she felt comfortable returning when she needed support.

Turning Endings into Referrals

Creating Positive Associations

Celebrate Their Growth: *Ensure they leave with a clear understanding of their accomplishments and the changes they've made.*

Acknowledge Your Role Appropriately: Take credit for creating a safe space and providing guidance, but emphasize that the work was theirs.

Leave the Door Open: Let them know they can return if they need support in the future, whether for the same issues or new challenges.

Provide Resources: Give them tools, book recommendations, or other resources to support continued growth.

Handling Difficult Endings

When Clients Disagree with Ending

Sometimes you'll feel strongly that therapy isn't serving someone, but they want to continue. This requires careful navigation:

Explore Their Perspective: Try to understand why they want to continue and what they feel they're getting from the sessions.

Be Honest About Your Concerns: Share your

observations about the lack of progress or poor fit, while remaining supportive.

Offer Alternatives: *Suggest different approaches, reduced frequency, or referral to someone else.*

Set Clear Expectations: *If you agree to continue, establish specific goals and timelines for reassessment.*

When You Need to End for Your Own Well-being

Sometimes you need to end therapeutic relationships for your mental health or because of boundary violations:

Trust Your Instincts: *If working with someone consistently drains you or feels unsafe, it's okay to end the relationship.*

Be Professional but Firm: *You don't need to justify your decision extensively, but you do need to provide appropriate referrals.*

Document Appropriately: *Keep clear records of your decision-making process and any concerning behaviors.*

Consult with Colleagues: *Get consultation when*

making difficult decisions about ending therapy relationships.

Creating Your Retention and Offboarding Framework Regular

Assessment Questions

Ask yourself monthly about each client:

- *Are they progressing toward their goals?*
- *Do I feel energized or drained after our sessions?*
- *Am I the best therapist for their current needs?*

- *Are they engaged and invested in the process?*
- *What would serve their growth best right now?*

Creating Decision Trees

Develop clear criteria for retention vs. offboarding decisions:

- *What indicates good progress vs. stagnation?*
- *How long should you continue without significant movement?*
- *What are your scope of practice boundaries?*
- *When should you seek consultation about complex*

cases?

Building Referral Networks

Maintain relationships with therapists who have different expertise so you can make good referrals:

- *Specialists in areas outside your expertise*
- *Therapists with different approaches or styles*
- *Providers who take insurance if needed*
- *Group therapy or intensive program options*

What's Coming Next

In our final chapter, we'll discuss scaling your impact and building a long-term practice that serves you. We'll cover seasonal growth strategies, creating effective systems, and building a practice that gives you the life you want while serving your clients well.

Because ultimately, the goal isn't just to build a successful private pay practice - it's to build a practice that sustains you personally and professionally for the long haul.

"How you handle endings matters enormously. A good ending leaves people with positive associations with getting help and openness to seeking support in the future."

Chapter Action Steps:
✓ Review your current caseload - identify who's thriving vs. stuck
✓ Practice having one honest conversation about progress with a client
✓ Create your standard offboarding conversation template
✓ Develop a referral list for clients who need different services

Chapter 9: Scaling Your Impact

Building a Practice That Serves Your Life

After years of building my practice and consulting with hundreds of therapists, I've learned that the ultimate goal isn't just financial success or a full caseload. The goal is building a practice that gives you the life you want while allowing you to serve your clients at the highest level.

This final chapter is about scaling your impact without scaling your stress, creating systems that work for you long-term, and building a practice that sustains you personally and professionally for decades.

The Fall Launch Advantage

There's a reason I've been encouraging you to launch this fall, and it goes beyond just good timing. Understanding seasonal patterns in mental health can help you build momentum and plan strategically.

Why Fall is Prime Time

September through November consistently see the highest demand for therapy services:

- *People return from summer with renewed focus and energy*

- *Students and families settle into new routines, creating "fresh start" energy*

- *Adults start thinking about what they want to change or improve*

- *The upcoming holiday season brings up family and relationship issues*

- *There's a collective sense of new beginnings that comes with fall*

Business Advantages:

- *Less competition, as many therapists are just getting back into routine*

- *Higher conversion rates on consultations and inquiries*
- *Natural momentum that carries through the busy winter months*

- *Perfect timing to establish new client relationships before the holidays*

My Fall Launch Strategy

When I expanded my practice offerings, I deliberately timed launches for early fall. I created messaging around "investing in yourself this fall" and "using the natural energy of the season for personal growth."

The response was consistently stronger than launches at other times of year. It felt aligned rather than forced, seasonal rather than sales-driven.

What I've learned about seasonal patterns:
- *Fall launches create momentum that carries through winter*
- *Spring can work, but it competes with vacation planning and busy family schedules*
- *Summer launches often struggle due to vacation schedules and lower motivation*
- *Winter launches work for some services, but requires different messaging*

Creating Seasonal Growth Patterns

Instead of trying to maintain the same level of activity year-round, smart practice owners work with natural rhythms.

My Seasonal Framework

Fall (September-November): Growth Season

- *Launch new services or groups*
- *Ramp up marketing and networking*
- *Focus on filling your caseload*
- *Plan for the busy winter months*

Winter (December-February): Maintenance Season

- *Serve your full caseload consistently*
- *Maintain existing systems and relationships*
- *Do minimal new marketing*
- *Focus on excellent service delivery*

Spring (March-May): Planning Season

- *Assess what worked and what didn't*
- *Plan improvements and new offerings*
- *Do professional development and training*
- *Prepare for summer schedule changes*

Summer (June-August): Renewal Season

- *Take real vacation time*
- *Work lighter schedules if possible*
- *Do deeper planning for fall launches*
- *Invest in yourself and your relationships*

Building Seasonal Flexibility

Variable Scheduling: *Structure your practice to work more intensively during busy seasons and scale back during slower times.*

Service Rotation: *Offer intensive workshops or groups during high-demand periods, individual sessions during maintenance periods.*

Professional Development Timing: *Plan training and conferences during slower periods rather than when you're busiest.*

Systems That Scale

The difference between therapists who burn out and those who build sustainable practices often comes down to systems.

Essential Systems for Growth

Client Management System:

- *Streamlined intake and onboarding process*
- *Consistent scheduling and payment collection*
- *Clear communication protocols*
- *Efficient documentation workflows*

Marketing System:

- *Content calendar for consistent visibility*
- *Networking follow-up processes*
- *Referral tracking and acknowledgment*
- *Website and social media maintenance*

Financial System:

- *Regular financial monitoring and planning*
- *Automated expense tracking*
- *Tax preparation and planning*
- *Revenue forecasting and goal setting*

Professional Development System:

- *Regular training and skill development*
- *Consultation and peer support*
- *License maintenance and continuing education*

- *Professional relationship maintenance*

My System Evolution

I started with basic systems and gradually made them more sophisticated as my practice grew. The key was implementing one system at a time and ensuring each one worked before adding complexity.

Phase 1: Basic Operations *Simple scheduling, basic payment collection, minimal marketing*

Phase 2: Streamlined Efficiency *Automated scheduling, consistent payment systems, regular marketing activities*

Phase 3: Strategic Growth *Sophisticated tracking, multiple revenue streams, systematic business development*

Phase 4: Sustainable Impact *Refined systems that require minimal daily management, focus on high-value activities*

Creating Multiple Revenue Streams

While individual therapy might be your primary offering, creating additional revenue streams can provide financial stability and professional satisfaction.

Revenue Streams I've Developed

Group Therapy: *Monthly groups for specific populations generate additional income while serving more people.*

Professional Consultation: *Helping other therapists build their practices has become a significant part of my work.*

Content Creation: *Monthly resources for my Patreon community create ongoing passive income.*

Supervision: *Providing clinical supervision to newer therapists serves the profession while generating revenue.*

Choosing Revenue Streams Strategically

Align with Your Expertise: *Choose additional offerings that leverage what you already know and do well.*

Consider Your Capacity: *Don't add revenue streams that require significantly more time unless they're proportionally profitable.*

Test Before Committing: *Try new offerings on a small scale before making major investments.*

Maintain Quality: *Avoid adding too many streams to prevent the quality of your primary work from suffering.*

The Patreon Model for Therapists

One innovation I'm particularly excited about is creating ongoing value for other professionals through subscription-based content.

How My Patreon Works

Monthly Vault Drops: *Each month, I create comprehensive resource packages - like the Fall Launch Prep materials - that my subscribers can download and use immediately.*

Community Support: *Subscribers get access to a community where they can ask questions and support each other.*

Office Hours: *Regular virtual meetings where people can get consultation on their practice development.*

Resource Library: *Over time, subscribers build a comprehensive library of practice-building resources.*

Why This Model Works

For Subscribers:

- *Affordable access to ongoing support and resources*
- *Community of like-minded professionals*
- *Practical tools they can implement immediately*
- *Continuous learning and development*

For Me:

- *Sustainable recurring revenue*
- *Ability to help many more professionals than I could see individually*
- *Creative outlet for developing new resources*
- *Community of engaged professionals*

Scalability: *This model enables me to impact hundreds of therapists with fewer hours than traditional consultation.*

Building Your Legacy Practice

As you build your practice, think beyond just the immediate future. What kind of practice do you want to have in 5, 10, or 20 years?

Questions for Long-Term Planning

Professional Legacy:

- *What impact do you want to have on your profession?*
- *How do you want to be remembered by colleagues and clients?*
- *What contributions do you want to make beyond individual therapy?*

Personal Sustainability:
- *What kind of schedule and lifestyle do you want long-term?*
- *How can your practice support your personal goals and values?*
- *What would make this work sustainable for decades?*

Financial Planning:

- *What are your long-term financial goals?*
- *How can your practice support your retirement planning?*
- *What kind of financial freedom do you want to create?*

Impact and Growth:

- *How can you serve more people without burning yourself out?*
- *What systems and innovations could amplify your impact?*
- *How can you contribute to improving mental health care broadly?*

My Vision for Sustainable Impact

- *I want to build a practice that allows me to:*
- *Serve my clients at the highest level*
- *Help other therapists build sustainable, successful practices*
- *Create resources that improve mental health care accessibility*
- *Model what's possible when therapists value their expertise appropriately*
- *Maintain my well-being and continue growing personally*

This vision influences every decision I make regarding my practice development.

Implementation: Your 90-Day Launch Plan

Let's make this practical. Here's your roadmap for the next 90 days:

Days 1-30: Foundation
Week 1: Clarity and Planning

- *Complete the ideal client and messaging exercises from Chapter 2*
- *Write your niche statement and elevator pitch*
- *Assess your current systems and identify priorities*
- *Set specific goals for your fall launch*

Week 2: Website and Online Presence

- *Update your website with clear messaging*
- *Optimize your social media profiles*
- *Create content calendar for consistent posting*
- *Set up tracking systems for inquiries and conversions*

Week 3: Networking and Professional Relationships

- *Identify 20 potential referral sources*
- *Reach out to 5 professionals for coffee or phone calls*
- *Join relevant professional groups online and locally*
- *Update your networking materials and introduction*

Week 4: Systems Setup

- *Implement or improve your scheduling system*
- *Clarify your policies and fees*
- *Create email templates for common situations*
- *Set up financial tracking systems*

Days 31-60: Building Momentum
Week 5-6: Marketing and Visibility

- *Begin consistent content creation and posting*
- *Send introduction emails to potential referral sources*
- *Attend networking events or professional meetings*

- *Start building your email list with valuable content*

Week 7-8: Service Development

- *Finalize your service offerings for fall*
- *Create intake processes and onboarding materials*
- *Develop any group or intensive offerings*
- *Test your systems with initial clients*

Days 61-90: Scaling and Refinement

Week 9-10: Full Launch

- *Announce your services and availability*
- *Implement your fall marketing strategy*
- *Follow up with networking contacts consistently*
- *Monitor and adjust your systems based on what you learn*

Week 11-12: Optimization

- *Assess what's working and what needs adjustment*
- *Refine your processes based on client feedback*
- *Plan for continued growth and sustainability*
- *Set goals for the next quarter*

Measuring Success Beyond Revenue

While financial success is essential, true practice success encompasses much more.

Metrics That Matter
Client Outcomes:

- *Are your clients achieving their goals?*
- *Do you feel effective and helpful in your work?*
- *Are clients satisfied with their experience?*

Professional Satisfaction:

- *Do you look forward to work?*
- *Are you learning and growing professionally?*
- *Do you feel aligned with your values and purpose?*

Personal Well-being:

- *Is your practice supporting your life goals?*
- *Are you maintaining good physical and mental health?*
- *Do you have time for relationships and activities you enjoy?*

Community Impact:

- *Are you contributing positively to your professional community?*
- *Are you helping improve mental health care in your area?*

- *Are you mentoring or supporting other professionals?*

My Definition of Success

Success for me means having a practice that:

- *Allows me to do clinical work I find meaningful and effective*
- *Supports my financial goals without dominating my life*
- *Gives me flexibility to pursue other interests and relationships*
- *Creates a positive impact beyond just my individual clients*
- *Models sustainable, ethical practice for other therapists*

Your Next Steps

You now have the framework, tools, and strategies to build a successful private pay practice. The question isn't whether you can do this - it's whether you will.

Making the Commitment

To Yourself: Commit to valuing your expertise and charging accordingly.

To Your Clients: Commit to providing excellent service that justifies their investment.

To Your Profession: Commit to modeling what sustainable, ethical private practice looks like.

To Your Vision: Commit to building a practice that serves your life, not dominates it.

Taking Action

Start where you are, with what you have. You don't need to implement everything at once, but you do need to start.

Pick the one strategy from this book that most excites you and commit to implementing it this week. Then pick the next one and implement it next week.

Momentum builds on momentum. Small, consistent actions compound into significant results.

Staying Connected

Building a private pay practice can feel isolating, but it doesn't have to be. Stay connected with other professionals who share your values and commitment to excellence.

Whether through professional associations, online communities, consultation groups, or informal networks, surround yourself with people who understand what you're building and support your success.

Final Thoughts

Private pay isn't a dream. It's a decision. *A decision to value your expertise, serve your ideal clients, and build a practice that aligns with your values and goals. You have everything you need to make this transition successfully. You have clinical skills, life experience, and something unique to offer. What you now also have is the business framework to package and present what you do in a way that attracts your ideal clients and sustains you professionally.*

The mental health field needs more therapists who understand their worth and create practices that model sustainability and excellence. Your success doesn't just serve you - it serves everyone who needs what you have to offer and every therapist who needs to see that this is possible.

Fall is coming. The energy is shifting. People are ready for change. Are you ready to help them?

Conclusion

You've reached the end of this playbook, but you're really at the beginning of your private pay journey. Everything you need is here - the frameworks, the strategies, the scripts, the systems, and most importantly, the mindset shifts that make all the difference.

Take what resonates, adapt what needs adjusting, and trust yourself to know what's right for your practice and your life.

Your expertise matters. Your time has value. Your ideal clients are waiting for exactly what you have to offer.

Now go build the practice you've been dreaming of.

Conclusion

Your Private Pay Journey Starts Now

If you've made it this far, you're no longer just thinking about private pay practice - you're ready to build one. You have the frameworks, the templates, the scripts, and most importantly, the mindset to create a practice that serves both your clients and your life goals.
Let me be clear about something: this isn't the end of a book. It's the beginning of your transformation.

What You Now Have
Over the past nine chapters, you've gained:

A Clear Foundation: You know your why and your who. You understand that clarity beats creativity when it comes to building a sustainable practice.

Proven Systems: Every template, script, and strategy in this book has been tested in real practices with real therapists. Nothing here is theoretical.

The Fall Advantage: You have a specific timeline and the seasonal momentum to make this transition when conditions are most favorable.

A Complete Toolkit: From messaging frameworks to networking templates to client journey maps - you have everything you need to implement immediately.

The CEO Mindset: You understand that successful private pay practice requires thinking like a business owner, not just a therapist.

The Path Forward

Here's what I want you to do in the next 48 hours:

Choose one strategy from this book to implement this week. Not next month. This week.

Block time on your calendar for the CEO work that will build your practice. If it's not scheduled, it won't happen.

Connect with your support system. Whether that's the Private Pay Practitioners community, a consultation group, or professional colleagues - you don't have to do this alone.

Set your launch date. September 1st isn't arbitrary - it's strategic. Use the fall energy to your advantage.

What Success Looks Like

Six months from now, when you're working with ideal clients who value your expertise, earning what you're worth, and running a practice that energizes rather than drains you - remember this moment. Remember that you had everything you needed all along. You just needed the framework to organize it and the confidence to implement it.

The Ripple Effect

Your success in private pay practice doesn't just serve you. It serves:

Your Clients: Who receive better care because you're not burned out and resentful about your working conditions.

Your Family: Who gets the best version of you because your work life supports rather than undermines your personal life.

Your Profession: Which benefits when more therapists understand their worth and create sustainable practices.

Future Therapists: Who will see what's possible and build their practices accordingly.

When you transition to private pay successfully, you're not just changing your career trajectory. You're contributing to a larger transformation in how mental health care is delivered and valued.

Beyond This Book

This playbook gives you everything you need to build a successful private pay practice, but it's not the end of your professional development. Keep learning, keep growing, and keep refining your approach.
Stay connected with other private pay practitioners. Share what you learn. Help the therapists coming behind you. The more successful private pay therapists there are, the better it is for all of us.

My Final Thoughts

I've been where you are. I know the fear of leaving the "security" of insurance panels. I know the overwhelm of trying to figure out business systems while maintaining clinical excellence. I know the isolation that can come with solo practice and the doubt that creeps in when you're building something new.
I also know the incredible satisfaction of working with clients who choose you specifically for your expertise. I know the freedom that comes with setting your own

rates and policies. I know the energy that returns when your practice aligns with your values.

The journey from where you are to where you want to be isn't always easy, but it's definitely worth it. You have the clinical skills. You have the life experience. You have something unique to offer.

Now you also have the business framework to make it all work.

A Personal Invitation

If you implement the strategies in this book and build a successful private pay practice, I want to hear about it. Your success story might be exactly what another therapist needs to hear to make their transition.

The Private Pay Practitioners community continues to grow and thrive because therapists like you share their experiences, support each other, and prove that sustainable, ethical private practice is not only possible - it's the future of our field.

Welcome to that future.

One Last Reminder

Private pay isn't a dream. It's a decision.

You've read the book. You have the tools. You know what to do. The only question left is: when will you decide?

*I hope the answer is **today.***

Final Implementation Steps:

✓ Choose ONE template from the appendix to implement this week
✓ Schedule 2 hours for working through it completely
✓ Set a one-month reminder to review and refine your progress
✓ Share your commitment with someone who will hold you accountable

About the Author

D.J. Burr, LMHC, LPC, is a licensed mental health counselor and private practice consultant who has helped hundreds of therapists successfully transition to private pay practice. With over a decade of experience in the mental health field, D.J. has walked the entire journey from community mental health to building a thriving private practice.

Professional Journey

D.J.'s career began in community mental health, where he experienced firsthand the challenges of working within insurance-driven systems. His transition to private practice wasn't linear - it included time in shared office spaces, an attempt at rapid scaling with multiple locations and staff, strategic downsizing, working from home, and ultimately finding success in a focused private pay model.

This varied experience gives D.J. a unique perspective on what works and what doesn't in building sustainable practices. He understands both the clinical and business sides of practice ownership, having made most of the common mistakes and learned from each one.

Specialization and Expertise

D.J. specializes in addiction and recovery work, with particular expertise in sex addiction recovery. His groups focus on this specialized population, incorporating modules on codependency and trauma work. He is also trained as an EMDR (Eye Movement Desensitization and Reprocessing) therapist. This deep specialization exemplifies the niche approach he teaches other therapists to develop.

His recovery journey informs his clinical work and business philosophy, demonstrating how personal experience, when used ethically and appropriately, can become a professional strength rather than a liability.

Private Practice Consultation

Through his consultation work, D.J. has assisted therapists nationwide in developing successful private pay practices. His approach blends practical business strategies with clinical wisdom, consistently emphasizing sustainable practices that benefit both therapists and their clients.

He is the founder of the original Private Pay Practitioners Facebook group, which continues to thrive after eight years and now has over 14,000 members. In 2025, he founded the Black Private Pay Practitioners Facebook group to create a safe space for Black therapists navigating their unique private pay journeys.

These communities have become a vital resource for therapists transitioning to and succeeding in private pay practice.

D.J. is also the creator of the Private Pay Practitioners Premium community on Patreon, where he provides monthly resource packages, templates, and guidance to therapists building their

practices. His "vault drops" include comprehensive toolkits that practitioners can implement immediately.

Teaching Philosophy

D.J.'s teaching philosophy centers on practical implementation over theoretical concepts. Every strategy he shares has been tested in real-world conditions - either in his practice or through his consultation clients. He believes that therapists deserve to be compensated appropriately for their expertise and that sustainable practices create better outcomes for everyone.

His approach to practice building emphasizes:

Authenticity over perfection
Systems over hustle
Sustainability over rapid growth
Value-based pricing over fear-based discounting
Professional relationships over marketing gimmicks

Personal Approach

D.J. is known for his direct, practical communication style that cuts through industry jargon to provide actionable guidance. He believes that private pay practice isn't about being elitist - it's about creating sustainable businesses that allow therapists to do their best work while building lives they enjoy living.

His own experience with the isolation that can come with solo practice has made him passionate about helping other practitioners build supportive professional communities and maintain their well-being while growing their businesses.

Current Practice

D.J. currently maintains an online private practice specializing in sex addiction recovery, offering both individual therapy and group work. His practice serves as a laboratory for the strategies he teaches, ensuring that his guidance remains current and practical.

He also provides consultation to therapists making the transition to private pay, helping them navigate everything from messaging and marketing to systems and scaling. His consultation work focuses on assisting therapists to build practices that align with their values and support their long-term goals.

Beyond the Practice

When not working with clients or consulting with therapists, D.J. is committed to his recovery journey and personal growth. He understands the importance of practicing what he preaches when it comes to work-life balance and sustainable business practices.

His work in the mental health field extends beyond individual practice to supporting the profession as a whole. By helping therapists build successful, ethical practices, he contributes to improving the overall landscape of mental health care.

Connect with D.J.

D.J. continues to support therapists through his Patreon community, consultation services, and speaking engagements. He believes that the mental health field benefits when more therapists understand their worth and create practices that model sustainability and excellence.

For more resources and to connect with D.J.'s work, visit his Patreon community at **patreon.com/ privatepay,** or find him at **djburr.com.**

"The goal isn't just to build a successful practice. It's to build a practice that gives you the life you want while allowing you to serve your clients at the highest level. When therapists understand their worth and create sustainable businesses, everyone benefits - the therapists, their clients, and the profession as a whole."
- D.J. Burr, LMHC, LPC

APPENDIX

Resource Library for Private Pay Success

This appendix contains all the templates, guides, and checklists referenced throughout the book. These are the same resources I provide to my Patreon community and use in my consultation work. They're designed to be practical tools you can implement immediately.

APPENDIX A: Assessment & Planning Tools

A1. Ideal Client & Messaging Clarity Guide

1. Grounding in Purpose

- Why are you pursuing private pay?

- What drew you to this model of practice?
- What are you no longer willing to tolerate in your business?
- What lived experiences or values make you uniquely positioned to serve your ideal clients?
- How do clients experience you differently from other providers?

2. Ideal Client Clarity

- What keeps your ideal client up at night?
- What are they afraid will happen if nothing changes?
- What do they want most (in life, relationships, or therapy)?
- What do they believe about themselves that might be getting in the way?
- What makes them feel seen, safe, or empowered?

3. What They Say vs What They Need

Complete the sentence:

- **They say they want_____, but they really need.**
- **They think the problem is_____, but the real challenge is_____.**

4. Your Voice & Positioning

- What kind of tone do you naturally speak or write in? (Calm, bold, nurturing, direct?)
- What are 2–3 things you stand for in your work?
- What are 1–2 things you actively reject?
- What do people often thank you for, or say they remember about you?

5. Messaging Practice Prompts

Try completing these:

- I help_____ who are_____ so they can_____.
- Clients don't hire me for_____, they hire me for___.
- The real reason people stay with me is because___.
- My work isn't for everyone — and that's a good thing because_____.

6. Pulling It All Together

Draft a short statement that reflects your clarity:

- Who you help
- What makes your approach effective
- Why your work matters

This can become your elevator pitch, bio intro, or homepage headline.

A2. Prequalifying Ideal Clients Guide

Why Prequalifying Matters:

- Saves time and reduces burnout
- Increases alignment and retention
- Positions you as a confident expert, not a default option

Key Indicators of an Ideal Client:

- They understand and value your niche
- They are financially prepared for private pay
- They express clear goals and a readiness to engage

Red Flags to Watch For:

- Price resistance or trying to negotiate rates
- Wanting a 'quick fix' or unclear about therapy goals
- Asking if you'll bill insurance when you clearly don't

Suggested Prequalifying Questions:

- What led you to seek therapy right now?
- Have you worked with a therapist before?
- What are your goals for therapy?
- Are you familiar with how private pay works?
- How do you plan to prioritize your time and financial investment in this work?

Consultation Structure (Suggested):

- 5 mins: Rapport + Clarifying Goals
- 10 mins: Needs Assessment + Fit
- 5 mins: How You Work + Fees/Policies
- 5 mins: Questions + Next Steps

Reflection Worksheet:

1. What qualities do I value in an ideal client?
2. Which types of cases drain my energy?
3. What boundaries do I need to hold firm during consultations?
4. What signs tell me someone is a great fit?
5. What's my go-to script for letting someone know we're not a match?

A3. Practice Assessment Worksheet

Current State Analysis:

Financial Health:

- Monthly gross income: $_____

- Monthly expenses: $_____
- Net profit margin:_____ %
- Target income: $_____

Client Demographics:

- Current caseload size:_____
- Ideal caseload size:_____
- Average sessions per client:_____
- Client retention rate:_____ %

Time Management:

- Hours per week on clinical work:_____
- Hours per week on business tasks:_____
- Hours per week on marketing:_____
- Vacation days taken last year:_____

Gap Analysis: What needs to change to reach your goals?

Clinical:

- Do you enjoy your current client mix?
- Are you working in your areas of expertise?
- Do you feel energized or drained by your work?

Business:

- Are your systems efficient?
- Is your marketing attracting ideal clients?
- Are you pricing appropriately for your expertise?

Personal:

- Does your practice support your life goals?
- Are you maintaining good boundaries?
- Do you have adequate support and supervision?

APPENDIX B: Marketing & Networking Templates

B1. 7 Ways to Boost Private Pay Referrals

1. **Get Clear on Your Niche** Be specific about who you help and how. Clear messaging makes it easier for others to remember and refer you. Action: Write a one-sentence niche statement: "I help [who] with [what] so they can [result]."

2. **Build Strong Professional Relationships** Prioritize connections with colleagues who share your niche or serve clients in complementary areas. Action: Aim for 1–2 outreach attempts per week: post in professional Facebook groups, set up coffee chats.

3. **Make Your Website Referral-Friendly** Include a clear description of who you help, what services you offer, and a simple way to contact you. Action: Add a 60-second video introducing yourself, or create a downloadable tip sheet for visitors.

4. **Attend Networking Events with Intention** Attend professional gatherings that align with your ideal clients or potential referral partners. Action: Commit to 1 new networking event in the next month.

5. **Provide Value First** Think about how you can support new professional connections before asking for referrals.

Action: Brainstorm three specific ways you can offer value to each new connection.

6. **Leverage Existing Professional Groups** Stay active in associations, local or virtual therapist groups, and listservs.

Action: Choose one group you're already in and plan 1–2 meaningful interactions each week.

7. **Showcase Your Expertise with Free Resources** Offer downloadable one-sheets or quick-tip resources on your website.

Action: Pick one simple resource idea you could create and upload this month.

B2. Fall Marketing Script Pack

"Back to Therapy" Social Media Templates

Template 1: Fresh Start Energy "September feels like a natural reset, doesn't it? If you've been considering

starting therapy, now may be the perfect time. Fall energy brings clarity about
what we want to change and the motivation to take action.

I'm currently accepting new clients who are ready to [specific outcome your therapy provides].

Sometimes the hardest part is just making the call. What would feel different in your life if you took that first step?
#therapy #mentalhealth #septemberreset #privatetherapy"

Template 2: Seasonal Transition "Fall transitions can bring up so much - excitement, anxiety, grief for summer, anticipation for what's ahead.
If you're feeling overwhelmed by change or unsure about your next steps, you don't have to figure it out alone.
I work with [your ideal client] to [specific outcome].
Currently accepting new clients for [timeframe].

Ready to invest in yourself this fall? DM me or visit [website] to get started."

Consultation Call Scripts

Opening the Call: "Thanks for scheduling this consultation! I have about [time] to talk today. Before we dive in, can you tell me what's prompting you to consider therapy right now? What would you most want to see change or improve in your life?"

Explaining Your Approach: "Based on what you're sharing, it sounds like [summarize their concerns]. I work with a lot of people who are experiencing similar challenges. My approach focuses on [brief description of your method/style]. What I find most effective is [key elements of your work]. Does that resonate with how you're thinking about addressing these concerns?"

Boundary Scripts for Increased Demand

When Your Schedule is Full: "Thank you so much for reaching out. I'm currently full with a waitlist, but I'd be happy to provide you with referrals to other excellent therapists who might be a good fit. I also offer [alternative - groups, intensives, etc.] if you're interested in those options. Can I send you some referral information?"

For Rate Shopping: "I understand that cost is an important consideration. My rate reflects [brief explanation - specialization, experience, private-pay benefits]. I want to make sure you find the right fit both clinically and financially. I'm happy to provide referrals to other qualified therapists who may have different rate structures if that would be helpful."

B3. Networking Accelerator Templates Email Templates for Professional Referral Sources Template

1: Reconnecting with Past Colleagues Subject: Quick Fall Check-in + Practice Update

Hi [Name],

I hope you're having a great start to fall! I was thinking about you and wanted to reconnect.

I wanted to share that I'm now offering [specific service] for [target population]. Given your work with [their specialization], I thought there might be opportunities for us to refer to each other.
I'm currently accepting new clients in [states] and would love to be a resource for you if you have clients who might benefit from private pay therapy.

Would you be open to a quick 15-minute coffee chat (virtual or in-person) to catch up and see how we might support each other's practices?
Best, [Your name] [Contact info]

Template 2: Introducing Yourself to New Contacts

Subject: Introduction - [Your Specialty] Therapist in [Location] Hi [Name],

I'm [Your name], a licensed [credentials] specializing in [your niche] in [location]. [Mutual connection] suggested I reach out as someone who might be a good referral connection.

I work with [ideal client description] and offer [services you provide]. I'm passionate about [what drives your work] and have availability for new clients.
I'd love to learn more about your practice and see if there are ways we can support each other's work.

Would you be interested in a brief introduction call? Looking forward to connecting, [Your name] [Your website] [Phone number]

Template 3: Following Up After Meeting Someone

Subject: Great meeting you at [Event] - Let's stay connected Hi [Name],
It was wonderful meeting you at [event/location] [timeframe]. I really enjoyed our conversation about [specific topic you discussed].

As I mentioned, I specialize in [your area] and work with [target clients]. I'm always looking to connect with professionals who serve similar populations in complementary ways.

I've attached a brief overview of my services. I'd welcome the opportunity to learn more about your work and discuss potential collaboration.
Feel free to reach out anytime if you have questions about private pay therapy or if you encounter clients who might benefit from my approach.

Best regards, [Your name]

Social Media Templates

LinkedIn Connection Request: "Hi [Name], I enjoyed [where you met/what you have in common]. I'm a therapist specializing in [your niche] and would love to connect with other professionals in our field. Looking forward to staying in touch!"

Instagram Story Templates:

- "Grateful for my referral partners who trust me with their clients 🙏 #privatepay #therapy #mentalhealth"

- "Fall is a great time to strengthen professional relationships. Who's someone you should reconnect with? #networking #therapist"

- "Reminder: I have availability for new clients specializing in [your niche]. DM me for referrals! #therapy #[yourniche]"

Follow-Up Message Templates

Template 1: After Initial Connection Subject: Following up on our connection

Hi [Name],

Thanks for taking the time to connect earlier this week. I appreciate you sharing insights about your practice and client population.

I wanted to follow up with [specific thing you offered - referral list, resource, article].

I'm here as a resource anytime you have clients who might benefit from [your specialization]. I'll also keep you in mind for [what they mentioned they do]. Looking forward to staying connected! [Your name]

Template 2: Quarterly Check-in

Subject: Quarterly check-in + practice updates

Hi [Name],

Hope you're having a great [season]! I like to reach out to my referral network quarterly to stay connected and share any practice updates.

Current availability: [Your current capacity] New offerings: [Any new services or groups] Ideal referrals: [Specific types of clients you're seeking]

How are things going in your practice? Any changes I should know about?

Always here if you need a consultation resource or have questions about private pay approaches.

Best, [Your name]

Tracking Your Network Categories:

- Hot Leads: Active referral sources
- Warm Connections: Professional relationships to nurture
- Cold Prospects: New contacts to follow up with
- Collaborators: Potential partners for groups/ workshops

Information to Track:

- Contact information and preferred communication method

- Specialization and ideal clients
- When you last connected
- Referrals sent (both directions)
- Personal details that help you connect
- Follow-up reminders and notes

APPENDIX C: Implementation Checklists

C1. Group Therapy Launch Checklist

6-8 Weeks Before Launch

Legal & Ethical Foundation: ☐ Review state licensing requirements for group therapy ☐ Update professional liability insurance to include group work (if applicable) ☐ Create group therapy informed consent forms ☐ Establish emergency procedures and crisis protocols for group sessions ☐ Confirm HIPAA compliance for group therapy settings □ Draft group confidentiality agreements for members

Group Structure & Planning: □ Define group focus/population (anxiety, trauma, life transitions, etc.) □ Determine group size (ideal: 6-8 members) □ Set session length and frequency (weekly, bi-weekly) □ Choose group format (open vs. closed enrollment) □ Plan group duration (8 weeks, 12 weeks, ongoing) □ Create intake/screening process for group members

Business Logistics: □ Set group therapy fee structure and payment policies □ Update website with group therapy offerings □ Create group registration system □ Plan waitlist management for group spots □ Prepare marketing materials for your group

3-4 Weeks Before Launch

Marketing & Outreach: □ Announce group on social media □ Send announcement to referral network □

Create informational content about group benefits ☐

Schedule consultation calls with interested clients ☐

Begin accepting registrations

Session Preparation: ☐ Plan first three session outlines ☐ Prepare group guidelines handout ☐ Create member contact sheet template ☐ Gather necessary supplies/materials ☐ Set up meeting space (virtual or in-person)

Final Preparations

First Session Ready: ☐ Prepare detailed first session agenda ☐ Plan icebreaker activities ☐ Create group norms discussion outline ☐ Prepare contact information collection method ☐ Review crisis intervention procedures

Launch Week

Day Before: □ Send reminder email to all members □ Double-check all logistics □ Prepare materials and space □ Review member information

First Session Day: □ Arrive early to set up □ Welcome each member personally □ Follow your planned agenda □ Collect feedback at session end □ Schedule follow-up if needed

Post-Launch (After Session 1)

Immediate Follow-up: □ Send thank you/recap email to group □ Address any concerns that arose □ Update marketing based on what you learned □ Plan session two based on group dynamics

Ongoing Success: □ Weekly session prep and planning □ Regular check-ins with group members □ Track attendance and engagement □ Adjust format as needed □ Plan for group transitions/endings

C2. Launch Week Action Plan

7 Days Before Launch

Morning (9-11 AM): ☐ Review all launch materials one final time ☐ Confirm any guest expert or collaboration details ☐ Update website/social media with launch information ☐ Send final reminder to your email list

Afternoon (1-3 PM): ☐ Prepare launch day social media posts (draft and schedule) ☐ Double-check all registration links and payment systems ☐ Organize physical materials (if applicable) ☐ Send personal messages to key referral sources

Evening: ☐ Review tomorrow's schedule and prepare mentally ☐ Set out clothes and materials for launch day ☐ Get good rest - you've got this!

Launch Day

Morning (8-10 AM): ☐ Post launch announcement on all social platforms ☐ Send launch email to your subscriber list ☐ Text/call your closest supporters for accountability ☐ Monitor early responses and engagement

Midday (12-2 PM): ☐ Engage with comments and messages promptly ☐ Share updates in relevant professional groups ☐ Post behind-the-scenes content (stories, reels) ☐ Check registration numbers and payment processing

Afternoon (3-5 PM): ☐ Reach out personally to warm leads who haven't responded ☐ Share success metrics if appropriate ☐ Address any technical issues immediately ☐ Continue engagement on social media

Evening (6-8 PM): ☐ Post end-of-day update or reflection ☐ Thank early supporters publicly ☐

Plan tomorrow's follow-up activities □ Celebrate your courage to launch!

Days 2-7 After Launch

Daily Tasks: □ Post educational content related to your launch □ Follow up with people who showed interest but didn't register □ Continue engaging with comments and messages □ Monitor and track key metrics

Crisis Management Checklist

Technical Issues: □ Have backup payment method ready □ Communicate issue transparently on social media □ Provide alternative contact method □ Document issue for future prevention
Follow up with affected people personally

Low Response Issues: □ Don't panic - launches often start slow □ Increase personal outreach efforts □ Consider extending registration deadline □ Ask supporters to share your content ☐ Review messaging to ensure clarity

Success Metrics Tracker

Quantitative Metrics:

Social media reach:_____
Email open rate:_____
Website traffic:_____
Consultation calls booked:_____
Registrations/sign-ups:_____
Revenue generated:_____

Qualitative Metrics:
☐ Quality of inquiries (good fit vs. poor fit) ☐
Engagement quality (comments, shares, messages) ☐
Referral source response ☐ Personal energy/
confidence level ☐ Overall community response

C3. 90-Day Implementation Plan

Days 1-30: Foundation

Week 1: Clarity and Planning □ Complete ideal client and messaging exercises □ Write your niche statement and elevator pitch □ Assess current systems and identify priorities □ Set specific goals for your fall launch

Week 2: Website and Online Presence □ Update website with clear messaging □ Optimize social media profiles □ Create content calendar for consistent posting □ Set up tracking systems for inquiries and conversions

Week 3: Networking and Professional Relationships □ Identify 20 potential referral sources □ Reach out to 5 professionals for coffee or phone calls □ Join relevant professional groups online and locally □ Update networking materials and introduction

Week 4: Systems Setup □ Implement or improve scheduling system □ Clarify policies and fees Create email templates for common situations □ Set up financial tracking systems

Days 31-60: Building Momentum

Week 5-6: Marketing and Visibility □ Begin consistent content creation and posting □ Send introduction emails to potential referral sources □ Attend networking events or professional meetings □ Start building email list with valuable content

Week 7-8: Service Development □ Finalize service offerings for fall □ Create intake processes and onboarding materials □ Develop any group or intensive offerings □ Test systems with initial clients

Days 61-90: Scaling and Refinement

Week 9-10: Full Launch □ Announce services and availability □ Implement fall marketing strategy □ Follow up with networking contacts consistently □ Monitor and adjust systems based on learning

Week 11-12: Optimization □ Assess what's working and needs adjustment □ Refine processes based on client feedback □ Plan for continued growth and sustainability □ Set goals for next quarter

APPENDIX D: Business Systems Templates
D1. CEO Time Blocker Template

Own Your Week Like the CEO You Are

Why Time Blocking Matters: • Shifts you out of reactive mode • Protects your high-value activities • Prevents business maintenance tasks from swallowing your day

Step 1: Identify Your Core CEO Activities ☐

Strategic planning ☐ Content creation ☐
Networking and marketing ☐ Financial reviews ☐
Systems improvement

Step 2: Template Your Ideal Weekly Schedule

Morning Block: • CEO strategic tasks (planning, marketing, financial check-ins) • High-energy creative work

Afternoon Block: • Administrative tasks • Email and communication • Professional development

Evening Block: • Client sessions (if applicable to your schedule) • Clinical documentation

Step 3: Protect Your Blocks • Schedule CEO time like client appointments • Turn off notifications during focused work • Batch similar activities together • Build in buffer time between activities

Step 4: Weekly Review • What worked well this week? • Where did you get pulled off track? • What adjustments need to be made? • How can next week be even better?

Sample Weekly Template:

Monday: Strategic Planning Day

- Morning: Business planning and goal review
- Afternoon: Marketing content creation
- Evening: Administrative tasks

Tuesday-Thursday: Client Focus

- Morning: CEO tasks
- Afternoon: Client sessions
- Evening: Documentation and preparation

Friday: Growth and Development

- Morning: Networking and relationship building
- Afternoon: Professional development

- Evening: Week review and next week planning

D2. Client Retention & Offboarding Flowchart

Why Retention & Offboarding Matter

Healthy private practices balance retaining great-fit clients and ethically offboarding those who have met goals or need different care.

Decision Tree:

Is the client aligned with your niche and expertise?
→ Yes → Proceed with retention steps
→ No → Offboarding may be appropriate

Is progress continuing toward goals? → Yes → Explore extending work → No → Reassess barriers; consider consult/supervision

Are sessions clinically productive and safe? → Yes → Retain and plan next phases → No → Consider referring out

Has the client reached their goals or plateaued? → Yes → Start conversation about progress and next steps together → No → Review and adjust treatment plan collaboratively

Retention Steps: • Regular progress reviews (monthly/quarterly) • Goal evolution and expansion • Celebrating achievements explicitly • Transparent communication about the value of continued work
Offboarding Steps: • Acknowledge the relationship and progress made • Explore their perspective on where they are • Provide appropriate referrals if needed • Leave door open for future support • Follow up appropriately after ending

Red Flags for Offboarding: • Multiple sessions without meaningful progress • Consistent lateness or missed appointments • Scope of practice issues arising • Poor therapeutic fit despite good faith efforts • Goals have been achieved and maintained

Retention Indicators: • Strong therapeutic alliance • Ongoing progress toward goals • Client engagement and investment • Complex issues requiring sustained work • Client expresses desire to continue

D3. Financial Tracking Template

Monthly Financial Dashboard

Revenue Tracking:
- Total monthly income: $____
- Number of sessions:____
- Average per session: $_____
- Other income sources: $_____

Expense Tracking:

- Office rent/utilities: $_____
- Professional liability insurance: $_____
- Continuing education: $_____
- Marketing expenses: $_____
- Technology/software: $_____
- Professional memberships: $_____
- Other business expenses: $_____

Profitability Analysis:

Gross income: $_____
Total expenses: $_____
Net profit: $_____
Profit margin:_____ %

Goal Tracking:

- Monthly income goal: $_____
- Actual vs. goal:_____%
- Annual income goal: $_____
- YTD progress:_____ %

Quarterly Financial Review Questions: • Are you meeting your income goals? • Which expenses provide the best ROI? • What financial patterns do you notice? • Where can you optimize spending? • What are your goals for next quarter?

Annual Financial Planning: • What was your total income this year? • What were your total expenses? • How much did you save/invest? • What are your financial goals for next year? • What business investments do you want to make?

FINAL IMPLEMENTATION NOTES

Getting Started:

1. Choose ONE template from this appendix to implement this week

2. Block 2 hours on your calendar to work through it completely
3. Set a reminder to review and refine it in one month
4. Add one new template each month until you have a complete system

Customization Guidelines:

- Adapt all templates to match your voice and style
- Modify timelines based on your capacity and goals
- Add or remove elements based on your specific needs
- Test small changes before implementing major overhauls

Ongoing Support: Remember that building a successful private pay practice is a process, not a destination. These tools are designed to grow with you as your practice evolves.

Most importantly: You already have everything you need to succeed. These templates help you organize and implement what you already know.

Private pay isn't a dream. It's a decision.

Now go make yours.

www.ingramcontent.com/pod-product-compliance
Lightning Source LLC
Chambersburg PA
CBHW071206210326
41597CB00016B/1692